ALBANIAN JOURNAL

For Ed and George —
at least the animals
seem to be content
in this devastated
country, though I
had a good time
there, as you'll see.

Happy holidays,
Mike
December, 1997

ALBANIAN JOURNAL
THE ROAD TO ELBASAN

EDMUND KEELEY

WHITE PINE PRESS • FREDONIA, NEW YORK

Publication of this book was made possible, in part, by grants from
the National Endowment for the Arts, the New York State Council on
the Arts and the Foundation for Hellenic Studies, a program under
the auspices of the American Hellenic Institute Foundation.

Cover photograph by Ron Padgett

Book Design: Elaine LaMattina

Manufactured in the United States of America

First Printing 1997

10 9 8 7 6 5 4 3 2 1

ISBN 1-877727-76-8

Published by
White Pine Press
10 Village Square
Fredonia, New York 14063

Acknowledgement

I am grateful to my wife, Mary, and my friends, John Chioles and Kay Cicellis, for their encouragement and advice on reading the first draft of this journal. A number of useful suggestions were provided by Bruce and Tad Lansdale, my faithful companions during part of the journey described in these pages. I am also grateful to other companions who contributed to the journal through their tolerance, generosity, and good humor on the road to and from Elbasan, and in particular to Christopher Merrill, who was not only responsible for some of the lightheartedness and hilarity recorded here but who subsequently introduced me to the journal's American publisher.

CONTENTS

June 27, 1995

The Mission

I've been invited by Tracy Cabanis, senior book production manager at Alfred A. Knopf, to join a group of American writers who will travel for a week in Albania under United States Information Agency auspices to meet Albanian writers, publishers, and journalists, among these one publisher in particular who visited the United States a year ago and who will be the group's principal interpreter and host, Bujar Hudhri of Elbasan. In addition to Tracy, the group will include the poets and teachers Brad Leithouser, Christopher Merrill, Ron Padgett, and Alan Ravage, all of whom are scheduled to arrive in Tirana by plane from Rome a few days before I would be due to arrive there by one of two weekly Olympic Airways flights from Athens.

The advance literature about the trip tells me that "the spirit of this encounter will be informal, personal, and down-to-earth, allowing for the open and spontaneous exchange of ideas and the forming of friendships among members of the literary market place" with the ultimate purpose of providing "a relatively simple and cost-effective opportunity for Americans to share in the movement toward Albanian entry into the world intellectual community." I find the language of this mission statement a bit disheartening, but more so is what I learn farther along: I would be expected to get myself inoculated against typhoid, tetanus, diphtheria, polio, and hepatitis, and I would have to be prepared to cope with Turkish-style toilets, with drinking only bottled water, with dressing for the heat of summer but also packing a jacket and tie for official meetings, and along with these, packing gifts of whiskey, chocolate, and books for our hosts, while keeping in mind that impoverished as the Albanians may be, they still have their pride. When I tell my Greek friends that I'm thinking of taking a trip to Albania, most warn me against it. "Why Albania? Even if the border is open now, it can't be safe to go there. Anyway, what's there that isn't here?"

All this makes me turn for courage and perspective to the journal of the English painter and poet, Edward Lear—probably more famous for his "nonsense" verse than his delicately representative landscapes—who decided some one hundred and fifty years ago to travel from cholera-infested Salonika through Macedonia to unfamiliar regions of Albania (he reminds us in the introduction to his journal that Gibbon called it "a country within sight of Italy less known than the interior of America"). Lear's mission at that time was to make "a large collection" of sketches illustrative of the landscape of Greece and Albania and to try and recover his health by a "change of air and place" after a severe illness in Greece had sent him to the banks of the Bosphorus for six weeks of convalescence.

On a mid-September day in 1848, he asks his dragoman-interpreter, Giorgio, an "absolutely necessary" companion for a journey of this kind, to get the horses ready. When they've been loaded with what Lear tells his readers are essentials for the trip—cooking utensils, a light mattress, a good supply of coats and plaids, two or three books, two sets of outer clothing ("one for visiting consuls, pashas, and dignitaries, the other for rough, everyday work"), rice, curry powder, cayenne, quinine pills, and of course "a world of drawing material," he and his dragoman set off on horseback at dawn for the unknown, which includes visits some two weeks later to Elbasan and Tirana, the two major cities on the USIA itinerary.

If a recuperating Edward Lear has the spirit to take his four post-horses along the mostly unexplored road to Elbasan in 1848, what possible excuse can I find for not accepting Tracy Cabanis's invitation to head the same way in the summer of 1995, especially with the promise of a minibus to serve our group as we may choose, surely an easier mode of access to adventure and discovery?

DEPARTURE

The Olympic Airways plane is one of those turbo-jet "commuter" kind that was recently banned in the States because ice forming on its wings brought one down this winter in the mid-West after threatening to bring down others here and there. My accidental companions for this flight, Bruce and Tad Lansdale, among my earliest friends from post-World War II Greece and now regular visitors to Albania to help set up agricultural schools there, assure me that there will be no icing problem in that newest of our shared countries, where the high mountains have been cleared of snow by the rising heat of what today seems likely to end up the hottest month of the summer, now over 100 Fahrenheit in Athens, about the same in Tirana. Still, ten minutes after we are settled into the crowded, simmering plane, the captain's voice comes over the intercom to tell us that we are to debark and await further instructions, for reasons left vague. Has news of the banning finally crossed the Atlantic to touch the hearts of those in charge of Olympic Airways? Hardly likely for hearts they say are shaped like the broken rings of their imitation Olympic Games logo.

The debarkation is halting, and a Greek gentleman who is clearly destined for a career in the local Parliament, rages at top voice against the stupidity, the indifference, in the last analysis, the cruelty of Olympic Airways for making their passengers suffer this kind of slow torture for an unnamed cause in a stinking, airless plane. The staff is half embarrassed, half sullen. In the waiting lounge there is a rush for iced drinks, sympathy from the hostesses on duty but no further news, no explanations. We wonder if Olympic is now on strike, a regular threat in the peak summer months that usually dwindles into a merely aggravating slowdown. Since the only other flight into Tirana this week is two days hence, we have no choice but to wait in ominous silence or go home. Nobody goes home. I find myself wondering if anybody ever goes home from an airport on impulse after debarking as we have—even with the excuse of an airport run by Olympic Airways. Or does flying out once the process has started, at least flying out into unknown territory, carry with it the same piercing thrill of inevitability as going into battle?

Within the hour we are suddenly back in the plane and rising into the clouds over Parnassus. There is cool air in the plane now and clear sky ahead. No one talks or moves the length of the plane, except the man in the seat across the way who is still shaking his head over the huge dark stain on his immaculate linen pants that he received, on boarding the second time, when a young lady speaking no recognizable language—Albanian, Slavo-Macedonian, Bulgarian?—turned suddenly to say something to her unshaven companion behind her and struck the arm of this clean-cut stranger next to her so that her brimming cup of Nescafe frappe fountained out in a long thick arc to land on his elegantly angled thigh. He shrugs now and says under his breath to nobody in particular: "What can one do after all? Can one expect anything else from the barbarians surrounding us?"

ARRIVAL IN TIRANA

The landscape on descending goes by too quickly to show how it differs from the familiar mountains and plains of Northern Greece, but the runway is clearly original: octagonal sections of concrete linked by asphalt, like a field of giant tiles laid out rather casually. There is a long row of concrete pillboxes beyond the outer rim of the runway, not the same as the low rectangles the Germans left behind in postwar Greece but mushroom-shaped, and lined up in close formation. Bruce and Tad explain that these are a remnant section of dictator Enver Hoxha's 1968 version of the Maginot Line, a network of some 700,000 pillboxes facing enemies real and imaginary across the border to the north, south, and east, but especially to the west, ready for those who might come by sea, including the Americans. What now seems to me a purely insane gesture, the architectural embodiment of Hoxha's gross paranoia, may once have had the subtler motive of providing the visible excuse for a harsher authoritarianism mid-way through Hoxha's Stalinist regime and the further isolation of an already desperately isolated country. It may also have provided work, however idiotic, for builders and soldiers otherwise unemployed, though, Bruce points out, the pillboxes were often manned by women raising children at home as best they could between shifts on guard duty. And each pillbox apparently cost more than it would have cost to build a reasonable house to take the place of the cramped and dingy two-room apartments that all Albanian families not part of Hoxha's entourage were forced to live in from one generation into the next.

Some days after this initial encounter with the pillbox network, I learned from our Albanian host, Bujar (pronounced "Bouyar") Hudhri, that his first shock of recognition about the total superfluity of Hoxha's defense line facing the western sea came when he discovered, during last year's visit to New York, that few Americans he ran into knew for certain exactly where Albania was on the world map. Most took it to be an East European country, while one sweet lady in the book business actually asked him if Albania had a coastline with decent beaches or was landlocked like Russia. "America our enemy?" he chortled. "America doesn't know we exist."

The driver sent to meet us runs swift interference to get us near the head of the passport line so that we escape the bottleneck created by official entries recorded and copied in careful script by two patently bored women civil servants dressed in dark clothes, as though left over from a late '40's movie. Our driver dips under the rope barrier to help the baggage handlers carry in the hand-delivered baggage. "We'll be late for our lunch with the Ambassador if we don't hurry," he says in a remarkably good version of American English. I don't ask him what Ambassador. I compliment him on his English and ask him instead if he's been to America, maybe working on a ship, like some young Greeks I know. He stares at me. "You are joking. What ship? I learned to speak American from the cinema."

LUNCH WITH THE AMBASSADOR

We're out of the airport in time for a drive through the city and a quick stop at the American Embassy compound on one of its far outskirts. The architecture of Tirana does not surprise me: it is as dreary as the reports have said, mostly faceless apartment buildings of bare brick and rough cement, the balconies—sometimes of brick, sometimes of cement—crude, incongruous, the smaller houses peeling and unkempt. The streets seem to me in better condition than the somewhat out-of-date *Blue*

Guide leads one to expect but not clean enough, though cleaner than the courtyards between apartment buildings, where a confusion of trash and garbage is at liberty to gather and move around as the unencumbered rhythms of nature dictate. I am told that there is no state system of garbage collection for such communal territory and no voluntary cleanup because the government is too poor at this time to pay for that kind of public service, and voluntary service, having become synonymous with forced labor under the Communist regime, is now gleefully shunned.

Bruce and Tad point out some of the city's landmarks: the Hotel Tirana, refurbished to handle international travellers and currently about as expensive as any in the Balkans; the Palace of Culture, a Soviet designed mess in concrete but on this day handsomely advertising a production of Tosca; the old-fashioned, tree-shaded Hotel Daiti, with the single public telephone available to travelers on its side of the city; the Enver Hoxha Memorial, what might pass close up for a modernist structure of sharp planes narrowing to a peak but from a distance appears to be an otherworldly creation that has fallen from on high to crash into the heart of Tirana at a weird angle. Apparently it used to house a sitting marble statue of dictator Enver Hoxha—Bruce reminds me that his name is pronounced "Hodja," like the highly entertaining mullah of Turkish jokes, Nasraedin Hodja—a statue once surrounded, they say, by all Hoxha had ever touched. But, as the gods inevitably arrange these things in time, the monument has now been emptied totally of Hoxha and has become the home of the Soros Foundation, USAID, and the United States Information Agency. Blissful children can be seen sliding down it steep facade to challenge gravity.

The Embassy compound on Rilindja Ridge at the edge of town is surrounded by a fence and has a guarded entrance. The barrier opens to a hillside with two rows of unpretentious but well-appointed two-story houses separated by well-kept lawns. In any other city, there would be nothing remarkable about this gathering of neat homes, except, maybe, its separate system of water purification and its clear contrast to the grubby university dormitories and other rundown residences that present a spreading vista of the still dispossessed citizens below its heights. The compound was evidently the Albanian government's idea, a way to insure that there would be no occasion for international embarrassment during the years when thievery suddenly became a national resource. Some of those living in the compound say they would prefer to be nearer the center of the city's normal life, that there is no longer the same threat in the streets that came after the Communist collapse. Others are grateful for the security and the ease, whatever their isolation from the real world outside the compound. It is a familiar foreign service story, but at the moment it is not our concern. We wash up in the house where the Lansdales are guests of an Embassy friend, drink cool water from the tap as usual, go our way. It is the last tap water I will taste for nearly a week.

Lunch with the Ambassador turns out to be lunch with the Greek Ambassador to Albania and his Cultural Attache at the Piazza Restaurant. The food is mostly Italian, the service Balkan, the bottled water Greek, the wine Albanian, the languages and interests at the table an equally mixed menu. The Americans—Bruce, Tad, Cynthia Caples, our Public Affairs Officer, and me—all speak Greek, but the Ambassador prefers to speak in English, though his Cultural Attache apparently speaks only Greek and is unfortunately seated beside the one Albanian present, Piro Misha, Soros Foundation director and President of Albanian PEN, who speaks English well but no Greek.

The Ambassador is urbane, engaging, vague, in spirit already on his way to another country and a new assignment, though he eventually expresses his enthusiasm for better cultural exchange between Greece and Albania, say through the presentation of a Greek film series under his embassy's auspices. "For Greek speakers in Albania or Albanian speakers in Albania?" Piro Misha asks, quietly, subtly. The Ambassador says, "Ah, alas, there are no Greek films in Albanian." Cynthia translates for the Cultural Attache. He lowers his eyes to his plate. Bruce brings him to life again by telling him a Nasraedin Hodja story in Greek. At the mention of Hodja, Piro Misha gazes across the table at Bruce. I explain that Bruce has in mind Nasraedin Hodja, the Turkish mullah and infinite source of comedy, who has nothing to do with your unfunny, murderous bully of recent history whose name happens to be pronounced the same way. Piro Misha smiles, less than whole-heartedly it seems to me. Is it the language barrier or just my language?

I ask Piro about Albanian PEN, which I have been told is alive and well. "If it isn't maybe what it should be, and it isn't, that's my fault," he says. "I don't have time to serve two masters, PEN and the Soros Foundation, and I would like the sec-

ond to support the first. That is what you Americans call a con-
flict of interest, no? I suppose I should resign, I think in
September I will resign—the presidency of PEN, that is." I urge
him to help keep his local PEN chapter active whatever his personal situation, especially since I understand that some foreign
and Albanian journalists have felt threatened recently, and the
famous local novelist, Ismail Kadare, now living in Paris, has
pointed to important human rights issues in Albania. "I understand he returned recently to protest the imprisonment of a former president and two former prime ministers, all at one time
rivals of the current president, Dr. Berisha. Am I right about
that?" Piro Misha smiles again, less ambiguously. "Kadare could
be president of this country," he says. "He is the most respected
Albanian. But he is above politics—too honest, too objective, I
suppose." He looks away. I decide to let politics rest until I have
a better grasp of what a foreigner in this country can and cannot comfortably ask someone he has just met, though Piro
Misha seems to me as candid in language and gesture as one has
any right to expect.

Riding to Elbasan

I am about to fall asleep over my *Blue Guide* to Albania in the
USIA library when my fellow travelers arrive in a minibus late
in the afternoon. Tracy is as ebullient and affable as usual,
though she tells me the group is exhausted from a long day on
the road. Christopher Merrill, as good-looking as our mutual

friend William (still Bill to me) Merwin and a lot younger, comes over to introduce himself and to say that he loves the Greek poets, travels with my Ritsos translations in his suitcase, and has read *Cavafy's Alexandria* twice. That, of course, makes for instant friendship, firmed up in the days ahead when we share stories about the pleasures and horrors of the writing life and discover the unsparing ironist and the secret juvenile delinquent that both of us carry inside us. On the trip south to Elbasan, I find that the other writers in our group—Brad, Ron, Alan—are each thoroughly amiable, accessible, game for what comes. The mood seems right, as it had better be given the close quarters in our bus and the hard roads ahead. As we leave the city and climb to the high ridge that appears to have been made just wide and flat enough to carry this rugged two-lane highway, our host, Bujar, moves in next to me and takes my arm. "Mr. Keeley. Look. Look at our country. Do you see our country? This is not New York. This is not New Jersey. This is not anywhere but Albania. Isn't it so?"

It is so, though I've seen something like it driving along the ravines of Kastania and Pelion and southern Crete. Here the tree-covered ridge opposite looks higher, the valley below deeper, the mountain ranges in the distance, one after the other, seeming to reach closer to infinite space. But the colors are the same, clean, primary, though the valleys are made up not of broad squares of yellow and green but of strips, narrow, short, telling of how little any villager owns these days even if that little—two and a half acres per family, they say—takes the place of the absolute nothing a farmer used to have under dictator Enver

Hoxha. It is "this magnificent mountain view" that most awak-
ened Edward Lear's lyricism, though he describes a more pris-
tine, uncultivated landscape:

> How glorious, in spite of the dimming sirocco haze,
> was the view from the summit, as my eyes wandered
> over the perspective of winding valley and stream to
> the farthest edge of the horizon—a scene realizing
> the fondest fancies of artist imagination! The wide
> branching oak, firmly riveted in crevices, all tangled
> over with fern and creepers, hung half-way down the
> precipices of the giant crag, while silver-white goats
> (which chime so picturesquely in with such land-
> scapes as this) stood motionless as statues on the
> highest pinnacle, sharply defined against a clear blue
> sky. Here and there the broken foreground of rocks
> piled on rocks, was enlivened by some Albanians
> who toiled upwards, now shadowed by spreading
> beeches, now glittering in the bright sun on slopes
> of the greenest lawn, studded over with tufted trees.

Lear's "progress" on his road to Elbasan was "of the very
slowest," often along "sharp narrow paths cut in the rock." Our
road is a puzzle of filled pot-holes, plugged in different seasons,
and the drivers who take it as it comes are fast, uncompromising until the last minute, carefree about death. The driver of our
minibus plays a game every now and then to tease Tracy, who
justly loves all things great and small: he goes for any living crea-

ture on the road—donkey, dog, turtle—to make Tracy scream and to give us a little thrill as he swerves clear of the creature at the last second, laughing.

But this driver knows the road and how to ride it, and we trust him not only because it becomes clear that he handles himself and the other drivers with authority but because the minibus is the one thing he owns and the source of his livelihood, purchased by way of Kosovo and Paris, where a Muslim compatriot of his worked out a deal with a Frenchman to make the brand new $30,000 car disappear so that the Frenchman could claim the loss of a new car from his insurance company and add to that reimbursement a donation of $5,000 from the driver's Kosovo compatriot, who then transported the shining minibus to Albania and sold it to our driver for a third of its original price. "Tell him that just ends up raising the price of the insurance we all have to pay," someone says to Bujar, hoping for a translation. Bujar glances out the window as though he hasn't heard. Around the next bend, he leans forward suddenly and says, "The castle. We must stop for the castle."

If you are brought up on gothic images it would be hard to see the gathering of rocks on top of the steep hill opposite as a castle that once housed the sister of the great fifteenth century hero, Skanderbeg, who united the Albanians against the Ottoman Empire and is said to have won twenty-five of the twenty-eight battles he fought against the Turks, evidently surviving the three he lost. The stones do take a certain recognizable shape as you reach them after a climb that curls around the hillside at an angle that takes the breath away but not with the sharpness you feel when you come up to the high point and find yourself on the edge of a cliff that falls straight down to the valley a mile below. The acrophobics, I among them, step back abruptly and lean against the remnant parapet wall. The others lounge on the cliff's rim to study or photograph the landscape that opens out from the Erzenit riverbed below and from the vineyards and orchards at its side to travel over range on range of purple mountains into that vague country to the south that surely must be Greece. As we walk the walls on the castle's safe side, Bujar speaks of Illyria and the Byzantine Empire that gave way to Albania's dark ages under the Slavs and that began to change with Skanderbeg's heroism against the Ottomans, only to end in our time with the dark age of Enver Hoxha. It is history I find hard to assimilate, and I think of Seferis's lines: "I've lived my life hearing names I've never heard before: /new countries, new idiocies of men /or of the gods."

Back in the circle of village houses below the castle hill, Christopher, Brad, and I, tired and thirsty, head for what looks like a taverna where there may be cold beer. They warn me that we have to be quick, or Bujar will insist on paying for our beer, as he has for every bit of food and drink that the group has consumed so far. We are not quick enough. By the time the rest join us, no beer has arrived and Bujar has inconspicuously ordered lunch, though it's almost six o'clock in the evening: a dish of mixed cheese and yoghurt, a deep bowl of tomatoes and greens, a plate of meat and potatoes, Albanian wine called—with touching optimism—Riesling, a cake set in syrup for dessert. A gang of young girls has gathered outside: they dance, they scream, they want their picture taken. Tracy lines them up and lets them mug their way through picture after picture. They want more.

The light of day is dimming as we leave our high road and head down to the plain that belongs to the town of Elbasan and its failed enterprise. The most dramatic image of its failure is the square mile of an abandoned factory complex that spreads in a dark brown stain across the valley. We learn that this rusting monstrosity once breathed out enough dark smoke to block the sun and cover the city and the plain beyond it with a gray cloud that confused the changing seasons. It was built by the Chinese some years ago to create an export industry out of concentrated ferrochrome, nickel, and other ores, the more abundant of Albania's natural resources, and it carried the name "Steel of the Party" after Enver Hoxha declared it the second national liberation of Albania. Thousands on thousands were transported to Elbasan to work its furnaces, with the tallest chimneys in the Balkans, but it never proved efficient enough to sustain itself with profit in the export market.

Some think the Chinese built the monster sloppily as a deliberate act of sabotage, others think the Chinese are sloppy by nature when it comes to industry, but all see it as Hoxha's grandest folly. Though one wing of the complex apparently still struggles to stay alive—as we pass by it breathes out a thin line of white smoke—we learn that the streets of Elbasan are filled with strollers the day long, young strollers (the median age in Albania is, implausibly, twenty-seven to twenty-eight) because the unemployed have nowhere to go now, and that has brought in a new pall to paint the town as gray as its architecture. That gray is relentless: workers quarters in concrete, public buildings in concrete, even the public squares mostly in concrete, and the streets a mix of dirt and cement, these to replace the prewar cobblestone streets, the ample public gardens, the gypsy merry-go-rounds. The change, they say, is partly the fruit of war, partly the fruit of Hoxha's great folly.

For those who can see things that way, it may also be a mysterious ghostly legacy from the distant past. Edward Lear, sighting Elbasan for the first time in 1848 "among rich groves of olives on a beautiful plain," found that beauty a deceptive halo over the town, which was "as wretched and forlorn within as without it was picturesque and graceful," with "dirty suburbs" and "dark narrow streets, all roofed over with mats." He concludes:

> The gloomy shade cast by these awnings did not enliven the aspect of the town, nor was its dirty and comfortless appearance lightened by a morose and wild look—a settled, sullen, despairing expression which the faces of the inhabitants wore. At length, thought I, these are fairly the wilds of Albania!

THE HOTEL SKAMPA

We are given an hour to clean up before dinner. I thought our late lunch was dinner, but I am told by my companions that so far the pattern has been five meals a day to accommodate the official and unofficial meetings on our schedule but also Bujar's abiding impulse to show, by way of friends and relatives, that Albanian hospitality, despite the current poverty, is what tradition says it is. Tonight we visit the home of one of his three brothers.

I decide to take the best part of our free hour to take a nap. My room is on the second floor facing the public square: what would be a modest room in a modest hotel in Italy, Greece, or Egypt, but here the fading furniture, the color of the sheets, and the stiffness of the towels gives the place the feel of a hotel room at the end of a long war and enemy occupation. The discoloration of the facilities in the bathroom is ominous, but the toilet turns out to be western, and in fact everything in there works, including the frozen pre-war shower-head and faucet assembly. The problem is that you have been warned not simply to avoid drinking the tap water or using it to brush your teeth but to keep it from touching your lips—surely an exaggeration, but nevertheless the source of some discomfort under the ancient shower-head.

The more honest discomfort comes, on lying down on top of the bed, first from the less than subtle hollow in the mattress, then from the rock-hardness of the pillow, but most of all from the blast of what seem to be local versions of once familiar rock tunes out of the loudspeakers set up to entertain the strollers and sitters who have taken over the public park below. I give up on the nap and sit up to attempt to write some notes on the day's trip so far, then give up on that because the mind seems to be passing through a dense gray cloud, a bad mixture of memory and lost desire. I go down to the front desk to ask the manager if there might not be a room on the other side of the hotel from the side facing the public square and its loud music. "Of course," he tells me in a respectable English accent. "You prefer to move to the other side of the hotel, we move you. Immediately. But you must know the rooms on the other side of the hotel have no bathrooms." I ponder the choice, finally dismissing the passing thought that no bathroom may, after all, be a blessing. "Thanks," I say to the manager. "I'll stay where I am." "Of course," the manager says. "In any case there will be no music by the time you return from dinner." I try to see if there is any half-buried irony in that remark, but the manager's face is the face of a rock cliff. I turn to find Christopher and Alan sitting in the lounge with several bottles of mineral water that they tell me is the only way to clean the spirit for what lies ahead.

What lies ahead is a visit to one of the standard two-room apartments that were the designated space for all Albanian families under Hoxha, except for those of high party officials during whatever span of time they happened to be in the dictator's favor. Bujar explains that he himself lives in the same kind of apartment in the same kind of standard apartment building but will soon be moving to an apartment with a third room, what we take to be evidence of his success as a publisher in the new free-market economy. As one has come to expect, there is a rich assortment of drifting trash in the apartment building's courtyard, but the apartment itself is immaculate. And if the living room becomes even more cramped than it usually is once the dining table has been moved in to accommodate the six of us, plus Bujar and our hosts, the place glows with the hosts' good will and their evident pride in the occasion, the daughters of the house, dark-haired, lovely, hovering in the doorway of the other main room to take orders but also to study, between dartings in and out from the kitchen, the shape and manners of these strangers arrived from another world.

Our manners—my manners and Christopher's in particular—leave something to be desired. We come bearing gifts of whiskey, chocolate, and books, as we were instructed to do by our advisors, and we engage in as much warm small talk as is possible through translation with a family we've never seen before and have some difficulty approaching on a first-name basis given the exotic sound of the names involved. And after the talk, we take to the sweet unidentified aperitif and the wine and the mutual toasting as though our thirst for such things is unquenchable at any time of day, do fill the glass again, thank you very much. Finally, with what heart we can muster at the hour of midnight, we get into the dinner that is now brought out in stages to delight us, first a mysterious thick soup of what must be grains with a meat base, then the tomato—cucumber—lettuce—olive—cheese—and I can't remember what else salad course, and we continue to do our best with certain wonderfully curious specialties meant to tide us over until the main course of two kinds of meat, sliced hard-boiled eggs on a base of greens, potatoes hiding another kind of chopped meat—please, no more, how do you say please no more in Albanian? I turn and whisper to Christopher, who is staring at his heaped-up plate as though it holds a sheep's head roasted on a skewer. How do you say please, didn't they tell you I was a vegetarian, for God's sake, Christopher says to his plate. We agree that there is no way we can get cleanly through that main course without resorting to the ancient Roman mode of relief, so we pick at it like spoiled children, hide things under whatever is leafy, and we take a pass on the dessert cake fully aware that this is a serious diplomatic blunder which we try to make up for by giving in thoroughly and heartily to the local custom of embracing and kissing everyone on both cheeks as we leave: the women, the men, the daughters.

In bed I fight against the puritan in me that broods on the waste that goes with such lavish hospitality in a country where so many people are still hungry enough to take the risk of crossing the southern border in search of sustenance and work where they are not welcome unless they can claim a degree of Greek ancestry and are under suspicion even then because of crimes committed by some of their more desperate or more villainous compatriots. What kills the puritanism is my sympathy with the old Mediterranean virtue of excessively generous gestures, still alive in small pockets of Greece but clearly thriving in the new Albania. And the air outside is cooler now and clear of music. I leave the window open. Something—the wine and good will, the sweet fatigue of discovering so much new territory, the charm of those attendant daughters—puts me into easy sleep on my first night in Albania.

JUNE 28

THE HOUSE OF ONUFRI

Breakfast at the Hotel Skampa is in a small private dining room that I assume is reserved for visitors from abroad because I get there only after the morning manager finds me searching for my companions in the larger empty dining rooms and guides me to the place I supposedly belong. Is this room a holdover from the days under Hoxha when foreign visitors were really special—the Russians for a while, then the Chinese, then nobody at all until the Italians, the European Union, and the Americans came in recently to help prevent famine? Maybe we are the only customers who can afford the hotel, even with the much cheaper rates that Albanians pay: $7.00 a night for a single room versus our $20. I did run into a group of local cyclists on tour coming down the hotel stairs with their bicycles on their backs and a young couple checking in at the desk. Maybe I don't know what I'm talking about.

The breakfast offered in that private room is not exactly a surprise: along with coffee and tea of several kinds, fried cheese, eggs, meats, and I can't bring myself to ask what else. I settle for a continental breakfast of bread, butter, and jam. We're on the road again by 8:30, in anticipation of a return trip to Tirana and a meeting with the Albanian Minister of Culture, but before that, we board our minibus and go around the corner to visit Bujar's publishing house, named after a famous 16th century icon painter, Onufri. Bujar is proud to tell us that his publishing house resides in a literal house that he bought to accommodate all his printing equipment and most recently his computer assembly that followed on his trip to the States last year. There is an almost life-size bronze-colored image of the painter Onufri in relief beside the front door of the two-story house, and Bujar has posted a guard outside the front gate, an ageing soldier dressed in an unrecognizable uniform that seems to be a hand-me-down from a local theatrical group. The guard is holding an unfamiliar rifle that Bujar suddenly takes from him, and the startled guard steps back in confusion. Bujar wants to show us that it actually has workable parts despite its antique history, but as far as I can tell, there are no bullets in it. Maybe the bullets are reserved for nighttime and weekends. Maybe bullets are beside the point.

Before we tour the premises, Bujar has us visit his upstairs office, where we sit in a circle to review and receive samples from his house list in exchange for some of our publications, left discretely on the coffee table. His assistant, Flutura Acka—whose new book of poems, *The Walls of Loneliness,* was celebrated in grand fashion, I'm told, earlier in the week—brings in a tray of small glasses that I take to be filled with orange juice but what proves in fact to be a very sweet orange liqueur with enough power in it to jolt you awake. I take this to signal the true beginning of another long and hazy Albanian day.

Bujar's enterprise is impressive in that it has grown from a print shop with one second-hand press into an establishment that apparently publishes some of the best new poetry and fiction in Albania and at the same time takes on printings for the state and commercial interests large enough to keep the enterprise in the black. The job in progress today is a book-length edition of the new Albanian customs regulations, a substantial contract that he won in competition with the best of the Tirana publishers.

During a tour of the working area, we learn that the equipment is still second-hand, imported from Greece, but he has several presses now, a heavy paper cutter, and all the computer equipment required to keep accurate accounts. He could use a book-binding machine, he tells us, because all his binding, even for uninteresting commercial texts like the customs regulations, has to be done by hand, including the use of a simple table fork to put a clean eighth-of-an-inch indented margin on the paperback cover of every book that comes out of Onufri. I promise to look into the availability of reasonably-priced book-binding machines when I return to Athens. Somebody else asks about the source of the paper he uses since paper of the right quality is evidently hard to find in Albania. Bujar opens a door and shows us pile on pile of what looks like some kind of rough stock. "Just in from Russia," he says. "The best we can do this month."

RETURN TO TIRANA

On the climb up from Elbasan to the ridge that carries us back to Tirana, I notice several crude mosaics some meters high in the retaining walls along the roadway. We go by these too fast for me to make them out clearly, but in one of the mosaics I can make out figures, men and women, carrying farm implements as though armed for battle. When I question Bujar, he shrugs. "Propaganda. Hoxha. Who cares?" I let that go for a while and listen to the conversation in the seat behind me: Brad questioning Ron, an expert on tennis history, about the qualities that made this or that player so remarkable in the past, and the prospects for this or that star on the current circuit. As a minor tennis addict, the conversation interests me and I learn from it, but something makes me want to get back to Enver Hoxha. Farther along I finally ask Bujar to give me, if he doesn't mind, a brief account of the Hoxha years. "What is there to say, Mr. Keeley?" Bujar says. I ask him, please, to call me "Mike," as everybody else calls me, since, for some reason, that is what my parents called me from the day I was born. "All right, Mr.Mike. "You want to know about the Hoxha years. They were terrible years. No outside friends, too little food, everybody afraid. This Hoxha, at an official meeting after he took power, walked up to his number one companion of the resistance days and in front of everybody killed him with his bare hands because this man disagreed with something our great leader was saying. Who after that would speak him? But what is worse, everybody believed him when he said we were surrounded by enemies from everywhere. Even the Chinese in the end. They betrayed us by receiving your Mr. Nixon, he told us. How could we have been so afraid and so stupid? Live for forty years the life he gave us and you would understand."

I decide to let it go at that, but Bujar, after glancing out the window for a long minute, turns to grip my arm again. He speaks his English slowly, as though each word is a phrase in a long sentence. "Let me tell you something else, Mr. Mike. I am not among the ones who now want revenge. Let history lie in peace. Let those who have a bad conscience live as they can with their conscience. And this means some now in the government and some in the opposition. Let the rest of us look to the present and the future. We need our energy for the problems we have in front of us. This is my belief." I decide I like this man. I put my hand over his and squeeze it.

The heat has begun to rise off the deep valley below us, and the mountain range that parallels our passage has taken on a light haze to mock our mid-morning mood. There is silence in the minibus until we head down into Tirana. Bujar says we now have an hour to spend before our meeting with the Minister of Culture, and he suggests a visit to a mosque in the center of the city, a mosque recently restored "because Hoxha cut off its head." It is not among the more famous mosques described in the *Blue Guide*, and as we approach it we see that the minaret, once presumably made of stone like all others, is now made of seamless concrete capped by a sharply pointed aluminum tower. Bujar appears to have chosen it to illustrate a sad bit of history. He tells us that this once important mosque—consider its central location—was converted to an "information" center under the Communists, the interior gutted and cleared of all remnant evidence of its original function so that it could better serve the needs of Party propaganda, distributed from this place in abundance to the dispossessed Muslim community, along with the deathless quota of decrees and regulations signed by Enver Hoxha or his ministers.

The interior of the mosque is fully carpeted now, the walls a bright white background to several hanging tapestries depicting Mecca, but the standard balcony where the women worshipers are meant to congregate in isolation from the men has not yet been rebuilt. The presiding holy man, with Bujar's help, gives us a brief account of the Communist persecution of Albanian Muslims that became especially severe after 1967, with the result that only some 100 of the then extant 1500 mosques in the country have survived to live again in the new Albania. As we leave, each of us is handed a bound copy of the Koran: the original text paralleled by a translation into Albanian.

We meet the Minister of Culture, Theodore Laco, promptly on the point of noon in his office on the top floor of an obviously important public building that has a dreary, unattended exterior, no interior charm, bad lighting, and no functioning elevator. Money for such amenities clearly does not exist. We are greeted warmly by the Minister himself, a suave-seeming man with middle-aged gray hair, who tells us—with the help of an eminent translator and companion of Bujar on his trip to the States—that he is himself a writer, in fact the author of eight novels, the last of which has just been released by Mr. Bujar

Hudhri's Onufri Publishing Company. The Minister says that he is especially pleased to be able to meet with us not so much on an official level as on the level of writer among writers. He motions us to take our seats in a kind of circle.

We are barely settled in when a tray arrives with large glasses filled with what I take to be a local version of the Greek "vissinada," a cherry-like fruit drink. One swallow stuns the throat: it turns out to be some kind of strong red wine. There are toasts. The Minister, now using his quite adequate English, pledges to do what he can to promote American writing in Albania, and we pledge to do what we can to promote Albanian writing in America. "Ah," says the Minister, "and I hope also writing by Albanians who have contributed to American culture." Have I heard correctly? I glance at Christopher, Christopher is glancing at Alan, Alan is glancing at Ron, Tracy is smiling broadly, Brad is glancing at Tracy. When Tracy suddenly raises her glass, we raise ours in a silent pledge to promote those Albanian writers who have contributed to American culture, whoever and wherever they may be.

More wine. The talk wanders. Christopher speaks to the Minister about the Albanian community that he discovered on passing through Worcester, Massachusetts, where he will move in September to teach at the College of the Holy Cross. The Minister already knows about that community, and he knows about others in America, in fact has visited some of them when he was last there (our advance literature for the trip provides the curious fact that Mr. Laco is an "American citizen because of his father," which may explain his apparent familiarity with the

United States.). The Minister finds that the Albanians in America are sometimes rude, suspicious. Not like Americans in general, we learn. "You are trusting people," he tells us. "We who have known so much cheating in our lives are not so trusting. We were once, I believe. No longer. Things have changed in Albania. Things have gone downhill. I mean in the way we look at life. Even since the end of Hoxha."

I find his candor disarming, also a bit unsettling. Is he really so much less of a nationalist than other Balkan officials I've come across, not least of all in Greece? Or are we being set up, courted for some purpose, robbed of our critical perspective by compliments, good fellowship, strong wine. This man is, after all, a member of Berisha's cabinet, and Berisha is thought by some to be well on his way to becoming a new kind of autocrat, good at finding ways to by-pass regular parliamentary procedures and even on occasion to jail those he takes to be a threat to his ambition. On the other hand, Bujar mentioned that this Mr. Laco had a reputation for fighting on the democratic side of things when it wasn't entirely safe to do so. Maybe I am misreading as political subtlety what is in fact a bit of honest social commentary by the novelist inside this member of Berisha's cabinet. In any case, the local wine has begun to go to my head in a warm rush unfamiliar at high noon, and that is enough to make me see this suave gentleman as among the more accessible public officials I've come across in my travels east of Rome and therefore deserving the benefit of my less than trusting American doubt.

We line up to shake the gentleman's hand heartily, with more pledges to promote cultural exchange between his country and our country and even countries to the south—my unsubtle contribution—and off we go our different ways only to meet the Minister again for lunch some minutes hence at the Mondial Restaurant, a clean, white-tableclothed place with cosmopolitan food. On the way there I ask Bujar to tell me a bit more about the Minister of Culture, where he came from in Albania, how he got into politics, and I learn that he grew up in a village not far from the Greek border, that he was an intellectual most of his life and only recently came into politics. "Like our Berisha," Bujar says, with a little smile. "A doctor most of his life, now a president."

I have enough wine in me to press Bujar about what he really thinks of President Berisha. "An honest man, I believe," he says. "But not a good politician." I don't press him further on that but turn to international matters. I ask him if Albanian intellectuals and politicians are as obsessed with the question of Northern Epirus and who it really belongs to as one still finds among some Greek intellectuals who have entered politics? Bujar looks at me. "Northern what?" I explain that I mean those regions in Albania near the border that were once part of greater Greece and are still Greek Orthodox in religion and still Greek speaking to some degree. Bujar shrugs. "Of course there are many Orthodox in this country, but what they speak other than Albanian I do not know. All I know is that we should love one another whatever we speak."

At the Mondial Restaurant our Public Affairs Officer, Cynthia Cables, has brought together enough Albanian writers and translators to fill several tables. I am eager to get away from politics and talk writer talk, but when the Minister of Culture arrives, looking cool and brightly washed, I find myself ushered around to the seat on his left, with no one on my other side. Fortunately Brad is seated opposite. Why doesn't he look as uncomfortable as I feel? I try to pull myself together, but some impulse, some remnant of the juvenile delinquent in me, makes me suddenly address the Minister in Greek. "Greetings. How are you? So nice to see you again." He stares at me. "Hello, sir," I say in English, smiling stiffly. "Just thought I'd try out some Greek," I say too heartily. "I was told you come from a village south of Korca, or what the Greeks call Koritsa, where a lot of people still speak Greek. So I've been given to understand. But I guess you aren't among them." The Minister is studying me. "It is true that I come from a village south of Korca, in fact only six kilometers from the Greek border. I can see the lake of Kastoria on the other side when the air is clear. But I speak no Greek." I'm still trying to smile. "I understand. I'm sure many people in that region don't speak Greek. And I don't mean to sound like someone who still thinks of that as Greek territory. I'm not a nationalist, so to speak. I'm not even Greek. One hundred percent American. I mean, the last thing I believe in is changing national borders."

The Minister is still studying me, then he reaches over for the bottle of white Albanian wine and fills my glass to the brim. "Of course my parents spoke Greek," he says finally. "In fact, wrote to each other in Greek. Because they learned to write in a Greek school, as was the custom at the turn of the century." I take a sip of the wine—only a sip, I tell myself, stay in control. "But not you," I say. "You didn't go to a Greek school. Or learn any Greek from your parents, right?" The Minister's eyes seem to smile very faintly. "Not me. Of course not. I went to an Albanian school. We all went to an Albanian school in my generation. We are Albanians, after all."

He turns now to speak in Albanian to the unidentified gentleman on his right and I focus on Brad. We talk of New York (I've been gone from the city since early May and something now makes me feel a pang of nostalgia): of our meeting several years ago at one of Galway Kinnell's lively dinners in the Village, of the joy and sorrow of writing for this or that New York review, of editors we have known who are no longer alive or active, of the state of publishing in America for aspiring or ageing poets and novelists. The latter talk turns me so somber that I finish my glass of wine and go for another.

RETURN TO ELBASAN

There is, thank God, ample time to doze during the late afternoon drive back to Elbasan, and since this is our third passage along the same mountain ridge, the landscape appears familiar enough to be refreshing without any longer startling your mind when you wake every now and then to glance at it. Forty-five minutes into the drive the minibus pulls over and stops. Tracy has an idea: to clear our heads we should stop and take a walk to the village on the far side of the road and maybe have a look inside a village home. Everybody sits up. We like that idea. We have yet to see the inside of village life. Bujar says he's certain the average villager would be honored to show his home to such distinguished foreigners, simple though the home may be. Tracy reminds Alan that he is unofficial group photographer, and Alan loads up. Those with a furry mouth take a long swig of mineral water.

As we head down a dirt side-road toward the village, I come up behind Christopher just as he suddenly moves a step to the right, hops on one foot, and with the other sends a rock in front of him toward an imaginary goal with a neat swinging kick that tells me he must be an old soccer player—not as old as I am by a long shot and more accurate with his stone than I could possibly be, but given to the same habit of taking a shot on goal with any object in front of me—stones, cans, plastic bottles—when the mood is right. I find out that he played for Middlebury College and has written a book about soccer. I admit to having played for Princeton in the spring of my freshman year while I was trying to toughen up my underweight body so that I could join the Navy very late in World War II. It was a time when my college class was a tiny remnant of its normal self, and Jimmy Reed, the short-legged but passionate soccer coach, was so desperate to fill his roster that he would take on anybody who knew that in soccer you dribble with your feet and keep your hands mostly to yourself, a thing I'd learned in the sandlot league of my pre-adolescence, while my father was serving as the American Consul in Salonika. When Christopher asks me what position I played, so many years have now gone by that I'm not sure I get it right. "Left outside," I say, wondering to myself if that is a mental slip designating how second-string I felt I was rather than a position on the field. Christopher is gentle. "The game has changed a bit and they don't use that term anymore. The positions are all more fluid these days, as you know."

What I know from my several recent excursions to the Princeton soccer stands is that the expertly crafted fluidity of the current college game has little to do with the game I knew, when Jimmy Reed would yell in distress at his backs—mostly disgruntled discards from the J-V football team—that if they couldn't learn how to kick the ball away, for God's sake, they could at least try to learn the subtleties of kicking their opponent. Christopher promises to send me his book, which was meant to help educate Americans about the joys and frustrations and skills of soccer, especially after America's entry into the 1990 World Cup and in anticipation of the 1994 World Cup that would take place in the U. S. and make the game accessible to anybody in America with a TV set. Given what I've seen of his wit and style, I can't wait to read it. He tells me now that the book was what is called a critical success but that the publisher dismally failed to exploit its potential market. I don't have to say "So what else is new?" We've been along that route already with poetry and fiction.

At the first farm house we come to, perched with a few others on a ridge above the gathering of houses that make up the village proper, Bujar motions us through the gate and goes up to the front door of the house to explain who we are. It is a house with a cleanly-plastered facade, sturdier than one might have expected, hard to see exactly what it's made of: probably a combination of brick and stone, though the stable-like structure at my side of the courtyard is made of mud bricks that were once plastered and whitewashed. Bujar comes back with the farmer, a man with a broad sun-tanned face so deeply lined that he could be over seventy but is surely some decades younger than that, with no trace of gray in his hair. Bujar tells us that the farmer's wife is sick, so we can't go inside the house, but the man would be pleased if we were to take a look around outside as freely as we choose. We feel a bit awkward about doing that but also a bit awkward about not doing that, so we follow the farmer to the plot of land by the side of his house where nothing I recognize is planted and to the orchard in front of his house where the strange fruit of mulberry trees stirs enough interest and complimentary gestures to eat up the time we need for a graceful departure.

We spend much more time at the next farmhouse on the ridge, where we find a fairly small, ancient woman in her forties sweeping clean her already carefully attended earthen courtyard. She beams when Bujar asks if we can come in. Her teenaged daughter at the well in the center of the courtyard turns away discreetly as we file in through the outer doorway. The lady of the house wipes her hands on her skirt and greets each of us in turn with a little smile and a single handshake, delicate but precise. There are chickens everywhere, flying chickens, the kind that, increasingly conscious of their ultimate destiny, have learned to rise as you approach and take off like flushed quail to land on the low branches of the nearest tree or beyond the wall that surrounds the courtyard.

We follow our hostess up the stairs of the main house and along the porch that leads to the living room, where we find spotless rugs and doilies and sofa coverings, the chairs humble but neat, the side-tables dusted and spread with things that have been newly washed or shined, as though the place has been readied for our arrival all along. This place tells another story from that of the Hotel Skampa and the dreary public buildings we've visited: maybe it speaks to the pride of personal owner-ship, or the return of traditional home-keeping, or the virtues of a self-sufficient life. Of course maybe the farm houses of Albania have always been as neat as this, ordered by the same sturdy pride that one found in the mud-brick villages of pre-war Greece.

It is difficult for me to reconcile this image with what we have heard about the extreme poverty of mountain villages in Northern Albania, where British visitors to the region after Hoxha's death were appalled to find farm families suffering from malnutrition and sometimes near starvation because they were unable to live on the quota of food left them after they had turned over to the state the prescribed and strictly regulated portion of their produce. Could they have known the same pride of place or given themselves to the same affectionate housekeeping? Something must have changed when the farmers there and here were given their own strip of land, even if a mod-est allotment by anyone's reckoning, and were then able to nour-ish to some degree their talent and their luck as they and the gods might dictate rather than Hoxha the Great.

I find myself brooding on politics again. I ask Bujar how these villagers have chosen to accommodate their post-war history and adjust to the new Albania. Do they talk about the past? Is there a remnant hatred, or disgust, or at least irony about what they were made to go through for almost fifty years? "Of course I cannot speak for most of them," Bujar says. "But let me show you something that says a thing about this family and others I have visited. It is something you and our American friends will not have understood." He walks over to one of the side tables and picks up an object that I take to be a curious bit of local handicraft strictly for decorative purposes since it is made out of paper leaves, hundreds of them, fanning out from a linked center—the linking a product of meshed folds—to shape something that you might take for an imitation lantern or lamp.

Bujar calls our group over and flips the leaves of this object with his thumb to show that they have printing on both sides: the unbound pages of a book or other printed matter rebound in this peculiar if well-crafted form. "You will find this nice lamp in many houses now," he says. "The laws and decrees of Enver Hoxha's government. These used to go to the people every week for necessary reading." He must think we don't believe him about this strange creation because he suddenly flips through the leaves again until he finds a page actually signed in print by Enver Hoxha. This he rips out, and then another and another so that each of us can take a leaf home as a souvenir. The lady of the house stands in the doorway watching, clearly amused— not at all proprietary, it seems, about her post-Hoxha artifact.

I'm told that city-dwellers manifested a similar post-Hoxha irony by taking home pages from his published writings wrapped around the vegetables they'd bought in the open public markets.

We move down to the courtyard again to have a quick look around the side of the house that is walled in by chicken pens and a low hut presumably for sheltering an absent farm animal or two because it gives off the sweet mixed odor of hay and dung. All is as carefully attended as the interior of the house. As we head back to the main gate our hostess suddenly stoops to scoop up a white hen who has strayed in too close to the woman's path, and she brings the furious squawking bird to Bujar, who cradles it in tight against his chest. "A gift for Tracy," he says. "We will chop off its head and take it with us to Elbasan." Tracy gasps, cries out, loses her cool, calls it unthinkable, mean, cruel, pleads with Bujar to leave the poor creature alone, then moves in to stroke its back as one would a cat and miraculously calms the bird down so that it suddenly stops squawking and settles for turning its head right-center-left, right-center-left, looking for a way out of Bujar's grip. Bujar says to Tracy, "But it is for you. For your dinner."

Tracy fixes him with narrow eyes. "Don't you dare." Bujar finally shakes his head and sets the bird down. It takes a short run and soars off into the nearest tree. Bujar turns and says something to the woman, something gentle—anyway enough, her expression tells us, to soothe her feelings about having her gift returned and to make for a diplomatic exit.

DINNER IN ELBASAN

Despite the minor clash of cultural mores occasioned by the chicken episode, the side trip into Albanian village life has put a glow on the day, only slightly dimmed by our descent into the factory-rich plain and dusty streets of Elbasan. It is twilight now. The strollers eager for action are again moving into the park beside the Hotel Skampa, the loudspeakers have come on strong with an Albanian version of "Love me Tender," and the air is thick with the days's remnant heat and the night's still unfulfilled expectations. We are due for dinner at the home of Bujar's assistant, Flutura, in an hour, and Ron, our trustworthy alarm clock, promises to walk the hotel corridor and rouse whoever needs rousing forty-five minutes hence.

I close my window and try to ease my way into a nap, but my brain is struggling to link too many random thoughts about the day's impressions, especially what I've sensed to be the contrasting aura of city and country life. I tell myself that I am no longer sentimental about the style of villages. I remember some years ago dismissing Henry Miller's nostalgia for pre-war rural Greece and his despair over what he saw—even if only from his post-war vantage point in Big Sur—as the disastrous progress that was turning the old stone and dirt paths into roads that could accommodate cars and trucks, along with the arrival of rural electrification that was rendering kerosene lamps and ice-boxes obsolete. Did he ask the Greek villagers who had been through three years of harsh enemy occupation followed by four years of equally harsh civil war in the '40s how they felt about coming out of those years to face the same back-breaking if simple life and the same isolation that they had known in the good old days? Could you blame them for wanting something easier, even if the cost was a possibly corrupting contact with the larger, meaner, more competitive world that would be likely to come to them with progress, as it eventually did to most villages that become towns on the main tourist routes, with their loud discos, bars, overpriced tavernas, and double-parked streets?

I now had to ask myself: if I had come to see an atmosphere of integrity and pride in the simple, unambitious village home we had entered, a resource that made up for what, at least on the surface, seemed to be missing in the streets and public buildings and apartment house courtyards of the two cities we had visited, was this a return to Henry Miller's kind of sentimentality that took too little account of what the Stalinist dictator Hoxha had put the country through and what the villagers themselves now wanted? On the other hand, did I have honest, unsentimental grounds for the anxiety I had begun to feel about the so-called democratic progress of local politics and the challenge to traditional values of the new market economy that were a product of Albania's increasingly rapid if still problematic effort to enter the late twentieth century under the supervision of the European Union and the United States? I am finally too tired to think clearly about these issues and give myself over to restless sleeping, only to be wakened in what seems less than ten minutes by Ron's knock on the door.

We meet outside the hotel with our evening's gathering of gifts, and head off on foot for our dinner rendezvous to see something of the town by night. Once we leave the cafés on the rim of the park beside our hotel, the town seems to be asleep, though it is not much later than normal dinner time in the Balkans. It seems dangerous to conclude that there is no night life in Elbasan, but that is the way it looks on this particular night, at least along our particular route. Flutura's place proves to be some distance from the hotel, far down one of the main streets, up another main street that leads to a branch of the local university in a rectangular building that looks as though it might do better for a branch of the local reform school system (if there is such a thing): barred windows, the panes often broken, and the yard in front a mine-field of scattered debris.

It is well after dark now, but few of the houses along our path have lighted windows, and in this section of town we are walking down the road alone. I think of Edward Lear's finding "melancholy" Elbasan "most oppressive after the pure mountain atmosphere," but I have no sense of the danger lying in wait that he must have felt after he forgot to wear a fez one day and was stoned by "knots of the Elbasaniotes" for doing the devil's work, first by sketching the town's principal buildings and then by "writing down" the local populace presumably in preparation for selling them to the Russian Empire. He concludes: "Alas! it is not a wonder that Elbasan is no cheerful spot, nor that the inhabitants are gloomy." At least our melancholy Elbasan seems quite benign. As we turn into a narrower side street, a bus, almost empty, comes around the opposite corner with a rattle in its ancient body that would clear the way ahead of all living creatures if any such happened to be around at this hour. It stops suddenly to let out a lady who has been sitting up front next to the driver. They wave gently to each other as parting lovers might.

Flutura's home is a surprise. It is not an apartment in the usual style-less structure of brick and cement but a detached one-story house with a garden in front. It reminds me of those small pre-war Greek houses, each with its garden and vined trellis, that used to lie along both sides Queen Olga Street, the main road into Salonika from the south, now lined by square apartment buildings four and five blocks deep. Flutura greets each of us at the gate with a double kiss on the cheek, introduces us to her parents and the other gathered members of her family, arranges us at the long table that has been set out on the pathway that divides the garden.

The night is clear above us and cool enough, but the group is unusually quiet now; serious fatigue appears to have set in after the day's long journey. Christopher and I share the foot of the table near the front gate, and we go quickly and heavily into the wine bottle that has been set more or less in front of us. We get through the soup course of delicious crushed vegetables without any trouble, and a just portion of the hors d'oeuvre dishes offering combinations of yoghurt and cheese and several not entirely familiar fried or boiled vegetables—squash, zucchini, eggplant?— to be dipped or doused in delectably unfamiliar sauces, along with slices of freshly baked bread. The salad course is also relatively easy because one can pick at that with a fork as infrequently as one chooses. But when the main course arrives with its meats, potatoes, sliced eggs, new vegetables and new kinds of cheese, I glance at Christopher and find that his eyes have turned subtle. He is watching Brad next to him. Brad is doing his duty, conversing as best he can with the gentleman on his far side, one of Flutura's relatives who speaks just enough English to be engagingly incomprehensible. Christopher moves quickly, depositing a piece of sausage and half a boiled egg on the edge of Brad's plate. I look beyond him as though I haven't seen what he is up to and spot an underfed dog ambling toward us from the corner of the garden. I encourage him to join us, using soft Greek animal-enticing sounds. He comes in to nip a bone-clean chicken thigh out of my hand and to carry it away. Christopher shakes his head at me to say that I have done wrong, then spots the house cat two chairs down the table, leans back and seduces it toward him with the promise of a batter-covered slice of veal.

More wine and fatigue go to the head. I turn to distract the lady sitting cater-cornered from me by telling her how much we are enjoying Albanian hospitality here in this home specifically but also in general. She has no idea what I am saying but smiles graciously, then turns back to take in Tracy's radiant amiability across the way and soon appears impervious to Christopher and me. It is our salvation. As news of our generosity spreads among the domestic animals of the region, some of whom are insatiable, it becomes difficult to hide our disgraceful behavior from our near companions, but it looks to me as though we make it through the main course without alerting our hosts at the other end of the table. And whether or not that is true, we surely earn some favor at the end by being the only foreign guests who have saved enough room after the fruit course for the syrup-drenched dessert cake that rounds out the meal.

I don't remember the walk home except that it seemed to me we closed out this long day by floating at a certain angle, as in a Chagall painting, a foot or two above the littered streets of Elbasan as we made our way back, and once home, by drifting easily into a dreamless sleep.

July 29

The Road to the Sea

By 9:00 a.m. we are in the minibus and on our way to the sea-side town of Vlora, once called Avlona by the Greeks. This is my first excursion outside Elbasan to the west, beyond the great factory graveyard and into the flat plain that takes us through one depressed village after another along the rugged highway to yet another depressed town. The latter are distinguished from the former only by the number of fading second-hand cars and trucks parked at irregular intervals along the road and the length of time it takes to clear the spread of ugly, unstuccoed brick and cement facades on either side of us. There are booths here and there displaying essential household products, but sparse evidence of other kinds of commerce and obvious signs of a prevailing poverty in the barren courtyards along the main road and the colorless clothes worn by those who sit or squat inside them to smoke a cigarette or two.

Before setting out from Athens what now seems days ago, I had a brief conversation with an Albanian journalist who was in opposition to the current government and sufficiently outspoken in print to think it wise to prolong his visit to Greece into

an indefinite future. When I asked him to give me some background on the Albanian economy, he said, "What economy?
There is no economy in Albania. Foreigners are afraid to invest
in us, and in any case we export almost nothing." I then asked
him how the government supported itself financially: was there,
for example, an income tax. "What income tax? How can there
be an income tax where there is no income? Families are meant
to live on sixty dollars a month. Sometimes several families." I
insisted that the government must collect some money from
somewhere. "Of course," he said. "By taxing imports.
Sometimes three hundred percent." The economics of that
taxed my understanding, but I could see from the dry provinces
we passed through this day that few imports at any price were
reaching the plains beyond Elbasan.

Throughout that morning I felt a return of the sentiment that
had first come on strong when I entered Elbasan and saw the
strolling unemployed: what price and how long were these poor
people supposed to pay for old political crimes that were none
of their making?

Early during our morning's drive we came to Pequin, Bujar's
home town. "You see, Mr. Mike, we still have our own Peking
even if the Chinese have left us to our fate." Bujar was clearly
the hometown boy who had made good; when we parked the
minibus and headed down the main street to pay a visit to the
local mosque, just about every fellow townsman we ran into
stopped to greet him, sometimes with a handshake but more
often with an embrace and a double kiss. "You should run for
mayor of this place," I told him. "No, Mr. Mike. I have told you.

I am an independent man. No politics in my life. Ever."

The mosque here had not suffered the same damage as the one we'd visited in Tirana, and what reconstruction there was did not violate its original stone facade. Inside, the wooden balcony that kept the women separated from the men was back in place, and the minaret, thought to be the highest in Albania, was now open to visitors. We climbed its narrow winding stairway to the walled-in balcony meant for the muezzin to call the faithful to prayer but as good a place as one was likely to find for a broad view of the wilderness behind us and still ahead. Bujar then led us across the way to the local remnant monument of ancient times, an undated castle that was barely definable as such because it had been brought almost to ground level by official pilfering under Enver Hoxha. Inside its truncated walls children now played what games they could without a ball or other equipment, and others apparently made use of one or another of its cell-like store-rooms for an outdoor toilet. Guarding a stretch of hollowed-out clearing along its outer perimeter—what may have once been a moat—crouched the concrete remains of a Hoxha bunker that the townspeople had not quite succeeded in smashing beyond recognition. At the far end of the clearing, a group of elders squatted in a rough circle over a game of dominoes.

We return to the minibus eager for the sea. It is still a long hour away, a fairly depressing hour that takes us through Lushnja, which the *Blue Guide* accurately describes as a "middle-sized industrial and commercial lowland town, with antiquated industries, poor housing, high unemployment, potholed roads."

It adds: "On first glance it is difficult to imagine that anything of fundamental importance to Albania could have happened here." To that I would add that the difficulty hardly clears up on second and third glance. Its importance, it turns out, was its role in rejecting policies put forward at the Versailles Peace Conference and in establishing national independence and a new political structure for Albania under the tribal leader Ahmet Zogu, who later became King Zog. It was also near this town that the Communist regime set up an important center for forced labor, condemning political prisoners to years of work on land drainage projects. The incidence of malaria in the region was once as high as 70 percent.

We learn why that was so as we approach the next depressed industrial town, Fier, which is surrounded by reclaimed marsh-land, once the prosperous breeding ground for the anopheles mosquito. As in the case of Elbasan, post-war industrial devel-opment—here in oil, bitumen, and chemicals—raised the pre-war population of 2,000 inhabitants to 75,000, but during our quick passage through its forlorn streets, it seems to be returning gradually to the small market-town economy of its origins. Either out of ignorance or our hurry to reach Vlore and a sea that we hope will cleanse our spirits of so many unholy images, we do not stop at Apollonia, one of the major ancient Greek sites in Albania now partially restored a few kilometers to the west—in fact, I for one do not learn how close we came to it until I return some days later to Edward Lear's account of his travels in the region. I'm embarrassed by having gone right by the site without even knowing it was there, my ignorance only a degree more excusable than the retsina-happy tourists I put into an early novel who skip a visit to the remnants of the Phaestos palace in Crete on the tipsy grounds of classicist authenticity: "After all, there weren't any ruins in ancient Greece," one of them says, filling his glass. And if Edward Lear ends up discovering in his day that the only remaining token of ancient Apollonia is a single Doric column on a dreary little hill, the rest having been removed by some local Pasha to decorate the town of Berat across the plain, at least Lear made the effort to go to the site and sketch what he could, though it meant crossing "a marshy flat tract, with scattered shrubs, throughout which concealed dogs rushed out with unpleasant abruptness from innocent-looking bushes."

There is new excitement as we come out to a sudden spread of fertile green that was once marshland, and in the distance beyond that, a glimpse of the dark blue sea, the Adriatic blue that circles Cefalonia, Ithaka, Corfu. Bujar says we will soon stop for a swim; he is in a vacation mood himself, having brought along his young wife and two-year old son to keep Tracy company in the front seat and to join us for lunch on the seashore. On the outskirts of Vlora, we stop by the local hospital so that he can speak to someone who presumably knows the best place to find broiled fresh fish. Christopher and I decide to have a look inside the hospital just for the hell of it.

This is a bad mistake. No one stops us going in through the side door close to where we park the minibus, and as we head down the wide corridor ahead—unlighted, in need of sweeping—we can tell from the smell and sound and general aura of this dark passage that the rooms we go by, some with doors ajar, are rooms where there is action: operating rooms, recovery rooms, rooms for the treatment of this or that injury, but not simply for the lying-in sick. I don't have the heart to look inside one of the open doors, but nobody would stop me from doing so, and I learn later that friends and relatives are sometimes allowed to attend those undergoing treatment and even surgery without benefit of masks or other standard precautions. I can't help wondering if they are there to assist the nurses or to bear vital witness on behalf of the dying patient.

Our pace quickens as we near the end of the corridor, with the main entrance ahead of us, and when we reach that we're halted by a guard who seems to mean business (is it my imagination, or is that a holster on his far hip?). He addresses us incomprehensibly but with authority. I smile broadly, Christopher smiles broadly, we tell him in one or another language he fails to understand that we mean no harm, gesture the same with what foreign gestures we know, and keep going. Uniformed—anyway partially uniformed—doctors and nurses gaze at us as we hurry out into the unmediated light. I glance back to see the guard behind us shrug and turn away. I remind Christopher of the standard hospital joke throughout the Balkan countries I have known: when they call the ambulance for you, go for a taxi as best you can, crawl to the street if you have to, and head straight for the nearest airport. I learn later from my American friends who live and serve in Albania that here this is no joke but an essential strategy.

The inner streets of Vlora are much like the desolate streets of our crossing so far, but as we come out to the seaside road, there is a hint of the particular quality of life that a resort town aspires to, here suggested by cafes near the beach and some of the paraphernalia for children and adults that goes with modern sun worshiping. But within the town limits, the beach itself is dirty: both the color of it and the refuse planted in it. And it is crowded by those hungry for cool water whatever their cluttered passage to it and by those lying out in small spaces cleared of cigarette packages, of discarded tissues, of rubber shapes of various kinds, of the tin, plastic, and glass remains of a developing sun-happy life. Bujar guides us farther out of town.

LUNCH BY THE SEA

The road leaves the principal beach area and climbs beyond the last of the seaside houses except two: just as we are about to enter a tunnel, Bujar tells the driver to stop so that he can direct us to a large if oddly bland concrete villa cut into the rock cliff below us on the right. "One of Enver Hoxha's summer houses," he tells us. "The place he took his few foreign friends. For a while." Then he points to another such villa above it on our left. "And that one belonged for many years to Communist Number Two, one Mehmet Shehu. Until he was murdered. You see, some of our former leaders lived very well for as long as they were allowed to live."

On the far side of the tunnel the road hugs the shore-line. The driver suddenly pulls over into a parking area behind a restaurant on the edge of a bluff that offers a clear view of Sazan island offshore to the west, and south of that, the long high arm of the Karaburun peninsula. It is there, or somewhere on the coast north of there, that the Americans have begun to set up an air base that will use pilotless airplanes to reconnoiter the war in Bosnia-Herzegovina—so a local rumor has it, subsequently confirmed by a dissident Albanian journalist, now in Athens, who was not allowed to attend the press conference that American military representatives apparently held to announce this surprising development. But at this moment that war couldn't be farther from our consciousness as we gaze down the shore to the south where grand shapes in water-dappled rock hover on the margin of a tranquil sea that shades out from the clearest emerald green to turquoise to the deep lapis-lazuli blue that most defines these waters.

Directly below is a small rock inlet with a patch of sand here and there, approached by a broken cement stairway. There is no discussion, no plan: Christopher, Brad, and I go for that access on the run, change on the beach, dive in and head out at a fast clip for the dark blue. The others follow. Alan comes in next, then Bujar in his jockey shorts, then his son in his, held at arms length by his wading mother. Ron has been carrying some bug that won't go away and decides to stay on shore to keep an eye on our scattered clothes. Tracy hovers at the water's edge undecided; she has no bathing suit. Suddenly she tells herself what the hell and goes on in fully dressed.

It is sea water as good as it comes: cool, buoyant, with the kind of clarity you think you can actually feel when you stop and hover to take in the water's touch full-length. We swim in pairs, go it alone, climb a rock in the sea to sit and talk, wonder what we have done to earn this sweet respite from our day's ambivalent journey, care not to think about it further and head off again in one direction or another to get our fill of this sea that the gods have chosen to grant us before the breath gives out. Two young men in bikinis have come out of nowhere to our patch of sand and sit on a boulder to watch Bujar entertain his son by twirling him so that his tiny feet skim over the water. They study Ron, then the rest of us out in the sea, obviously amused by these water-happy foreigners, especially when Tracy comes out of the shallows in her dripping dress and stands in a corner to brush the water off.

The driver on the bluff above us now signals that lunch is ready. The fish the waiter brings each of us in turn—fresh as it comes, broiled over charcoal, garnished with parsley, lemon, and olive oil—is not exactly a surprise in its seductive look or its superb taste, even if no one has the right language to identify it in English (something between a porgy and a local sea bass), but the size of it is surprising: each fish big enough for two. Bujar has overdone it again, and we struggle to show that we're grateful, the struggle growing larger when the salads and vegetables arrive but finally kept in manageable perspective by the old Albanian "Riesling" that we have come to know so well, here sharply chilled so that it goes down as easily as cool water and soon dilutes dissent. I pick my fish clean in due course and ask Christopher if I can have his fish-head. He slices it off and passes it to me without a word. "I don't eat the eyes," I tell him. "Just the cheeks. The most tender part." His look moves up from the fish-head to me. "That so?" he says. I loosen a cheek with my fork. "Absolutely. Because fish don't smile. The cheek is a muscle they never use." Christopher looks away, then back at me, then at my plate. I can see he thinks me unconvincing, light-headed, maybe a little weird. "Seriously, have you ever seen a fish smile?" I ask him. He shrugs. "No, but one of those fish-eyes just winked."

An Albanian couple has moved into a table down the way, and another joins them before their first course. Both men and women are dressed in brighter colors than we've seen during our morning's ride, and they are clearly ready to bring bounty to their table. City folk from somewhere, I say to myself. One of the women is quite pretty, maybe thirty-five, hair carefully bobbed—and far from the quiet reserve that we've found in the several hostesses who have invited us into their homes in Elbasan, she talks a lot at her companions and has a flirtatious way of flicking her hair to one side. The other woman at the table, a bit younger, seems as entertained by her as are the men. Like the girls and women of my awakening in early post-war Greece, neither of the two shaves her legs.

I am in vital need of a siesta after this meal, as is normal in those who are given to eating fresh fish for lunch by the Mediterranean Sea, but I seem to be the only one so desperate. Bujar brings each of us a bottle of Italian mineral water to clear the palate, and before we're fairly into that, he has us back on the road and heading farther south to show us a section of the coast that is known for its stretch of deserted beach. We can't go very far, he explains, because soon we will enter a forbidden military region, close to where there used to be a submarine base supplied by one or another of Hoxha's fleeting sponsors. What is in the region now, nobody knows, but there are rumors and rumors, especially since the very recent news that Greece and Albania have suddenly become friendly enough to conduct joint military exercises labelled as training for possible humanitarian relief missions.

The deserted stretch of beach proves less than deserted: a cafe at the end of the dirt road leading into it, and the beach itself mostly clear of casual debris but not of substantial abandoned hardware, what seems the legacy of a long-ago landing, even if the equipment is facing the wrong way. Among other disfigured relics, there is the rusty skeleton of a truck to our right and of a windowless bus to our left. But the sea is the same sea, and Brad, Christopher, and Alan go for it again, a safe distance south of the cafe. I take a walk in the other direction, looking for a place first to relieve my bladder and then to lie down. I use the truck skeleton for cover, then find a patch of hard sand and stretch out with my fisherman's cap over my face for as long as Bujar will grant me—about half an hour before we are back in the minibus and heading north through Vlore and Fier.

RETURN TO ELBASAN

Our destination now is the Albanian Orthodox monastery of Ardenica (pronounced "Ardenitsa") on a side road half-way between those uninspiring provincial towns of Fier and Lushnja. We climb through a village and wind our way up a steep hill to reach the monastery, and when we come out of dense foliage to the first lookout point facing the west, what we see below us is a landscape of gentle hills carpeted in green, and beyond that more unbroken green leveling out as far as the distant sea: marshland recovered by forced labor and once the principal source of grain, now uncultivated, some of it—fecund though it seems from this perspective—apparently returning to marshland. What adds a surrealist touch to this landscape, more in evidence here than anywhere else we've been, are the concrete pillboxes lined up irregularly row on row for miles to the right and left, like toadstools in some mad giant's abandoned playground. Bujar tells us that these, along with concrete tunnels cut into the hillside beneath us, were part of the elaborate system that Hoxha constructed in the 1970s to counter the expected nuclear attack on Albania by missiles fired either from Russia or from the United States, which explains why the pillboxes are sometimes facing east and sometimes west. However they may be facing, it would seem—my militarily knowledgeable friends tell me—that a sweep of fighter planes and a well-placed paratroop drop behind the nearest line of these concrete toadstools would render any section of that defense even less effective than the disastrous Maginot Line.

The monastery on top of the hill takes the visitor back to a somewhat saner age, under the protection of less threatening powers, visible and invisible. The church in the center, built originally in the thirteenth century and rebuilt in the eighteenth, the cypress trees around it, the cloisters and cells for the monks, all have a familiar Greek Orthodox aura. And as one finds in many Greek churches, built into this or that facade here are pagan remnants from a classical site nearby—in this case mainly from Apollonia, about fifteen kilometers to the south.

The duties of guarding this holy place are now unfortunately split between a priest who protects the church and its famous eighteenth century frescoes and a secular attendant who protects the church's bell tower and outer buildings. The priest has returned to the village below for his afternoon siesta and is unavailable, so we are limited to what little we can see of the frescoes—dark fragments only—from a single dust-coated window in the open porch outside the church's narthex. That is more than disappointing. We try to make up for it by climbing up a staircase and steep ladder to the top of the bell tower—which somehow survived Hoxha's violent attack on all religious structures—for a high view of the surrounding country and the road back home. Before heading that way, we look in on one of the cloisters, now converted into a quaint inn, with dining tables set out beside the arches of its inner wall. This commercial inn, open to the general public, is one thing that distinguishes this Orthodox complex from monasteries in Greece; another thing is the absence of a room near the entrance that some monasteries set aside for the sale of religious tracts and trinkets.

The light has begun to change as we reach the main road, but that does not much soften the image of torpid, grubby streets in Lushnja, Rrogozhina, and the villages that follow as we turn east for the last stretch home. Bujar, though now clearly as tired as the rest of us, tries to keep our interest alive by pointing out evidence of the growing commerce in foreign products, from flour to cement, trucked in from Greece or Kosovo or by boat from Italy. The sacks of this or that piled up by the roadside like sandbags only intensify the perception I have of a people too long and unfairly deprived.

At one point we go by an open butcher shop with a half-dozen newly skinned lambs hanging in a row. Somebody sounds the alarm about that—a ghostly echo of Edward Lear's encounter with Elbasan butchers and their "dogs, blood, and carcasses filling up the whole street and sickening one's very heart"—but we're well past the place before the driver figures out how useful those bloodied heads with bulging eyes and bared white teeth might be for exasperating the animal lovers among us, me included. Closer to Elbasan, we pass several horse-drawn wagons loaded beyond reason with hay or other produce, and Tracy asks our group photographer, Alan, to take a picture of that local excess if he gets a chance. Our driver still can't get the timing quite right but finally pulls up just after cutting around a hatless farmer with a face made of dark crocodile skin riding the front of his single-horse-drawn wagon overburdened with heavy greenery of some kind. Alan thrusts his camera out of the window to face the wagon, and when he clicks the shutter, the farmer makes his hand into a fist and then lowers it to his groin to masturbate the air in front of his fly—surely a more civilized response than the stoning that Lear, agent of the Devil, had to suffer for sketching people publicly in the Elbasan of his day.

During the trip's last miles the talk turns for a spell to literary politics back home. On one issue, the writers among us who have an opinion—Brad, Christopher, and I—appear to agree: prizes, grants, and fellowships in creative writing, government sponsored or otherwise, are not necessarily evil, as some rich and famous writers contend (along with Jesse Helms and his like), but they probably best serve not the established but the talented young and hopeful. This strikes me as a disinterested position considering the middle age median of those travelling in our minibus, though there is a fleeting suggestion that recognizing the unjustly unrecognized, however old the writer, may have merit as well. By the time we reach the dusky outskirts of Elbasan, there is silence in the minibus from front to back, Bujar's son finally asleep in his mother's arms, Bujar now out of things to reveal, the rest of us dozing or submitting to our own self-inflicted thoughts. On arrival we trudge up the Hotel Skampa stairs in disorder heading for our various rooms, stop to give our wake-up orders to Ron the tireless, then disappear into an hour-long oblivion.

Dinner is scheduled for 9:30 p.m. at the home of another of Bujar's brothers. We walk there again, in my case with simulated animation, a shorter distance from the hotel than the previous night's dinner but through streets and courtyards as cluttered with casual debris and as barren of charm. The apartment offers the familiar tight two-room allocation of family space, but the hospitality in it is as ample as ever. Bujar's brother proves to be a broad-faced, relatively portly version of his slender younger brother, with a jolly smile but no shared language and in any

case only a modest impulse to talk. His wife is generous in form
and gesture, his daughters younger and less inquisitive than
those who captured our gaze in the past, but equally efficient at
bringing in food.

The subtle pacing at the dinner table that I've mastered by
now works well for the first two courses, then seems about to
falter into obvious disclosure half-way through the third course
—a truly impressive heap of meats and eggs and potatoes—when
I happen to notice that Bujar has left this latest plate almost
untouched. I smile at him, questioning with my head. He smiles
back and makes a motion with his hand that I take to be the
Albanian version of someone being full up to here. This, suddenly, is liberation. I nod in full agreement, then carefully lay
down my fork. I feel I have an obligation to prod my ally
Christopher, who is quick to get the point: he smiles at Bujar
and his plate, sighs, covers his mouth with a hand to hold in an
appreciative belch real or imaginary, then lays down his fork in
a terminal position. Tonight it looks as though we're home free,
with good conscience.

On the way back to the hotel we break up into two groups,
Tracy, Bujar, and Alan some distance behind the rest of us who
are moving at a faster pace. We cross a patch of open ground
between converging streets, a crude triangle that serves for a
square where some of the unoccupied young meet to smoke and
presumably to plan the night's future. They don't seem threatening as we approach. In fact, they appear to care not at all who
we are or where we come from, barely taking us in as we pass in
front of them, their interest no doubt focussed beyond these

brightly dressed tourists on some darker and more enticing aspects of their town. I miss knowing what those might be.

As we reach the boulevard behind our hotel, a car of a certain age packed with young men comes swirling around the corner to our right and passes in front of us at a fast clip, hell bent for another world. Farther down the boulevard it swerves suddenly, careening onto the sidewalk and off again, then disappears around a far corner. Somebody in our group saw it go for a cat or try to miss a cat: wasn't there a thump, a squeal, both? We angle down the boulevard toward the back of the hotel. As we cross over to the park beside it, we spot the cat some distance away lying dead still in the middle of the road, what appears to be a stain of blood in front of its mouth. "That's that," somebody says. "Just don't tell Tracy." And that's the last thing said before we say goodnight.

JUNE 30

CHECKING OUT OF ELBASAN

We bring our bags to breakfast. This is our last hour in Elbasan, and for some the last day in Albania. In the morning we are to return to Tirana to be interviewed live on State TV, and in the afternoon Bujar, Flutura, and I will drive the rest of our group to the Rinas airport for their departure to Vienna. To fulfill my USIA contract, I am to stay in Albania through the weekend, but exactly where in Albania remains unspecified.

It is hard for me to feel sentimental about leaving Elbasan, and yet I recognize that, like Cavafy's Ithaka, poor as the town may seem, without it and the House of Onufri, there would have been no journey, no adventure and discovery, no excuse for setting out in the first place. I also find myself compromising about the Hotel Skampa: is it really that ghastly after all? I think of Edward Lear's mid-nineteenth century lodgings in the region, his overnight "khans": empty dark cells exposed to the street with a mat for a bed, the squalling of cats on one side of his pillow and the quacking of ducks on the other, sometimes with rats, mice, cockroaches, and lesser vermin for nighttime companions, or "huge flimsy cobwebs, hanging in festoons" above his head and "frizzly moths, bustling" into his eyes and face, while singing Gheghes squat outside his open doorway "murmuring their wild airs in choral harmony." In the face of that, how can one complain seriously about a sway-backed bed, faded furniture, archaic toilet fixtures, undrinkable water, and an Elvis Presley song in Albanian from the public park below—especially when it turns out that the hotel bill has already been settled?

That fact causes discussion. Bujar has paid this large bill for us, as he has all others for food and drink along the way, and he refuses to accept any reimbursement despite Tracy's efforts to persuade him that such expenses are covered by our per diem allowance. We decide to let the issue ride for the moment but to put together an envelope containing our individual per diem allocations to pass on to Bujar by cunning or violence as the group prepares to disperse in the afternoon.

Before heading north to Tirana we again visit the House of Onufri for a morning liqueur and a round of "Guzoya" toasts to everyone's health. Bujar has books to give us, and Flutura an inscribed copy of her poems, and Bujar's wife a different present for each of us, mine a wood-carving of two cream-colored birds with spread wings perched above each other on a brown branch. Those of us who have not yet contributed a recent book of our making to his library inscribe it and leave it on the coffee table. A degree of melancholy sets in as we say goodbye to the staff of Onufri and especially at the minibus door when we exchange farewell kisses with Bujar's gathered relatives who have opened their homes to us.

As we climb above the Elbasan factory, Bujar is singularly quiet, while others of us are engaged in reviewing future travel arrangements. I wonder if he is withdrawing back into the community of his own concerns, or if he feels we are. I decide to talk to him about the news he reported to us with some enthusiasm yesterday, on our way to the Ardenica monastery: our driver, he said, had heard over the radio that Albania had just been admitted to the Council of Europe. We'd celebrated the news with him without being exactly sure why we should. I now ask him what implications that development may have for local politics. "It is good for Berisha," Bujar says. "A sort of victory. That is why he spoke about it on the radio." I ask: but doesn't that mean Berisha will now have to conform to European standards in the area of human rights and democratic procedures? Bujar shrugs. "These standards are European. That is what is important. You see, we can now say that Albania is officially in Europe for the first time since before Enver Hoxha."

I look back for a final view of Elbasan and find that it has already vanished below the bend we'd just left behind us. I realize that it won't necessarily be the final view for me, because I have in mind joining my friends Bruce and Tad Lansdale two days hence for their return to Greece by way of the road that passes through Elbasan and continues on to Lake Ochrid and the southern town of Korca. But the town's going now feels final. Nobody speaks of that. We talk about Tirana and what lies ahead for us at the State TV studio. There are questions: who will be in charge, what will we be asked, what can we say and not say? "Do not worry about these things," Bujar tells us, laughing. "You can say whatever is in your head. I will be the interpreter, so I can make it come out right."

STATE TELEVISION

We arrive in Tirana right on schedule for our interview, but it turns out that a studio schedule in Albania is about as flexible as any schedule in the Balkans. Our morning cultural program is already in progress, we are told, and it will go on being in progress for some time, so there is no hurry. We wait to go into the studio, and once inside, we wait again. I sense a certain nervousness among those of my companions who haven't been before a TV camera recently, anyway in a context involving foreign languages. Bujar tells us not to worry, it is the middle of the day, our audience will be those with enough free time to be sympathetic. And besides, we are visitors, Americans—he doesn't say therefore possibly interesting curiosities, but I sense that implication.

The arrival of our interviewer doesn't much settle things down: she is a young, good-looking brunette, made up from head to toe, dressed to kill. I faced her likeness once in Athens, a young lady with acrophobia who was forced by her director to climb a rock outcropping of the Pnyx in high heels and miniskirt and conduct her swaying interview in a strong breeze on the edge of a precipice so that the Parthenon on the Acropolis behind us could appear cleanly in the frame's background. Here it is hard to tell if there is a director among the gathered cam-

era folk; it appears the interviewer herself is in charge of this seg-
ment of the cultural program. She asks if anybody would like a
drink of water. We all raise a hand. She then perches herself on
a high stool and curls her long legs elegantly under her. "You
want to know what I will ask you? I will ask you three questions
only: who are you, why are you here, what are your impressions
of Albania. Each of you can answer." We look at each other,
then we quietly agree that Tracy should answer the first two
questions succinctly for all of us and that we will then go for the
third in turn.

While the camera people are setting up and checking the
microphones, Bujar comes in to stand behind the interviewer,
hands folded in front of him, looking rather dolorous. We learn
why that is when a second chair is moved in beside the interviewer, and a long-faced, heavy-browed young man with collar-
length black hair comes in to introduce himself as our interpreter. His English strikes me as dubious at best, faster than
Bujard's but not as careful or as coherent. We learn that he has
recently moved to the New York area on some kind of graduate
fellowship and is presumably back in Tirana for the summer—
that is all we learn. The cameras are ready, the interviewer and
interpreter are ready, we sit there in a row waiting for the final
signal. At the last minute, Bujar moves over next to the interpreter and bends to say something to him. The young man
nods, Bujar smiles at us. "O. K.," he says. "I will help your interpreter"—a final shot of reassurance.

The interview goes well, at least from our side of the micro-
phone, the only side we can fully understand. Tracy introduces

us in turn and summarizes our mission in language that is a distinct improvement on the written charge we were given at the start of our trip: no mention of the market place or cost effectiveness. She introduces us simply as American writers who are here to learn about Albania's writers and publishers and to exchange ideas with them about how we can help each other. And she goes on to say convincingly what a pleasure working at that has been. When it comes to our impressions of Albania, each of us does his best to speak from the heart about this or that aspect of the life we've seen that has touched us. Brad, after saying that he doesn't really want to criticize his country while abroad, nevertheless proves eloquent in articulating our communal sense of America's rather provincial failure to know as much as it should about Albania and the Balkans in general, especially—and this he doesn't say—in view of the confusing role our government now seems to be to playing in the region. I go on too long about my delight in the landscape, in the hospitality and other old-fashioned virtues of many we have met—which I hope will not vanish as the market economy grows—in the work of writers like Ismail Kadare on behalf of human rights, and in the good prospects that should come with Albania's admission into the Council of Europe.

I'm vaguely conscious—my companions more so, I soon learn—that only a portion of what I've said has been picked up by the interpreter, despite Bujar's help. I blame that on my loquacity rather than the interpreter's limitations; others in our group suggest censorship, especially the glaring omission of Kadare's name. We begin to wonder just how much of what we've offered our hot mid-day audience was actually carried over into Albanian, and when Bujar confirms that the interpreter who was imposed on us not only left out a lot but constantly got things wrong, we go off to lunch at Cynthia Caples' with a certain feeling that we've been had by the State TV. Tracy says never mind, she loved what we said and the way we looked saying it. In the end, we settle for that.

THE FIRST GOODBYE

Lunch at Cynthia's is a generous buffet of hors d'oeuvres, sandwich makings, and drinks in the dining room, but some of us find that even looking at that kind of spread costs us what appetite we have left after these hard days and nights of Albanian hospitality on the road. And with the group and its hosts about to break up and travel in separate directions, the mood is tentative, in any case less than lighthearted. There is floating talk of books and writers in the living room, questions of future itinerary and final money exchange in the kitchen. Christopher comes up to me in the hallway complaining that in the room the women come and go talking of John Updike. "Our John Updike. Not the Albanian John Updike, for Christ's sake." We confirm summer and post-summer addresses. Suddenly Bujar tells us that it's time to go to the airport. For most that appears to be chilling news.

As we head out to the minibus Tracy asks me, since I will be staying on in Tirana, to serve as banker for the per diem money that will go to Bujar in an envelope. My free pocket begins to fill up with a mix of dollar bills and Albanian leks passed to me discreetly while we climb aboard and arrange ourselves in our usual seats, and after we make a quick stop in the center of town to change some gathered travellers checks, my pocket is bulging in a way that strikes me as at best embarrassing and at worst dangerous. When we arrive at the airport I hover behind to make a quick series of adjustments that distributes the wealth I'm carrying so it's less available to local pickpockets or incredulous authorities.

The airport is a mess, all doors blocked by uniformed guards, all passageways jammed by relatives and friends of the arriving or the departing. Bujar clears a corridor to the entrance door outside the check-in counter, but is held back there by a guard who is uncompromising: only those with passports are allowed inside. The farewell embracing with Bujar and Flutura has to take place outside, in the midst of the pressing crowd, quickly, awkwardly, with elbows active and epithets violent. I flash my passport at the guard and go on inside to shake hands with my companions and surprise Tracy with a farewell triple kiss. We decide that we are all going to meet again in New York City this fall. There will be "Guzoya" toasts, and photographs to share, and who knows? maybe plans for another trip to some other undiscovered country. Bujar is still half-waving from the doorway, disconsolate. As I turn to join him, Christopher says "Now don't you stay out of trouble just because I'm not around." I promise to do my best not to, difficult as it may be without his practiced if still precocious collusion.

I join Bujar and Flutura at the fence along the runway. We wait awhile, none of our people shows, so we give up and head back to the minibus. On the way into town Bujar grills me about my background, as though we're starting out on a new adventure. Do I think of myself as an American who is more Irish than anything else because that is my father's name even if his mother was Welsh, or more German because that is my mother's origin? I'm not in a mood to be expansive about that, so I say rather disingenuously that most Americans don't worry about their origins the way Europeans do, we're usually too much of a mix.

Bujar isn't convinced, but I move on to talk a bit about high points in the trip, and I tell him that what success we may have had was mostly his doing. "But Mr. Mike. This is not the truth. Why don't you speak the truth?" I tell him that as a writer it is my professional duty to try and tell beautiful lies, but in foreign countries while in the pay of my government, I always tell the truth and nothing but the truth. I indicate that it is a lesson in diplomacy learned from my father and brother, professional diplomats. "But diplomats lie," Bujar says. "That is their profession. Writers tell the truth." I tell him if that is so, then he has just made a liar out of me, a writer. "This is a problem," Bujar agrees. I then present him with the famous Greek conundrum: a Cretan writer says all Cretan's are liars. Since the writer is a Cretan himself, he must be lying, which means the truth is that all Cretans tell the truth—but that in turn must include the Cretan writer, who therefore must be telling the truth when he says all Cretans are liars. Flutura intrudes, "This makes me dizzy. Please, tell me some American poetry." I recite what I can remember of "Prufrock" and let it go at that.

Our farewell takes place in the lobby outside the USIA library, where I am to meet Cynthia, who has been good enough to offer me her guest room for the night—but our parting comes only after Cynthia has spent more than half an hour of ardent diplomacy both in English and Albanian persuading the reluctant Bujar that in truth he must accept the envelope I have prepared for him—with the USIA secretary's help—because not to do so would mean that our group would have to return our unexpended per diem allocations to the American government or be in violation of our USIA contract. In the lobby Bujar embraces me hard and long, as he does his brothers. I am touched. Flutura says goodbye sweetly but is not quite so forthcoming with her person. I watch them board the minibus. It turns to head off in the direction of Elbasan.

I try to read portions of the *Blue Guide* having to do with my route two days hence while waiting for Cynthia, inexhaustibly professional, to finish her afternoon's work. I find I'm too preoccupied, maybe too much into a letdown, and it doesn't help my mood when Cynthia conscientiously introduces me to a young internet specialist who has been hovering in her office and who now follows me out to the lobby and there, with the best of intentions, explains in truly overwhelming and incomprehensible detail exactly what state of the art computer equipment and programming he is in the process of introducing into Albania under some kind of government grant. Soggy-brained, I head for the men's room. The young man is still there when I get back, but so is Cynthia, and after they have gone over this and that official business that I manage to keep out of my hearing, Cynthia's driver shows up to take us off to the American Embassy compound on the Rilidja Ridge. Bruce and Tad, I discover, have moved into the house next door, guests of Deedee Blane, a highly accommodating lady who heads the local AID program. When they invite us over to watch some live Wimbledon on their hostess's TV, Cynthia takes a pass, but even low level Wimbledon interests me. I stay on to watch a cassette of "Rumpole of the Bailey," increasingly into withdrawal, and fall asleep half way through. For once, I have no hesitation about turning down dinner.

I find Cynthia in the living room checking something out on her laptop. We chat briefly, I excuse myself and head for the guest room. The sheets are a delicious dark blue, and the soft sturdiness of the double bed reminds me of home. Besides my wife Mary, all that is missing is my cat Salome, who sometimes sleeps at my feet. I think of Seferis and his cats, the source of her name. Then I think of Seferis serving as Greek Consul in pre-war Korca—which he called Koritsa—and the poems he wrote there. One of them begins, "There, you see, at last I love these mountains with this light /their skin wrinkled like an elephant's belly." That gives me a landscape to look forward to.

July 1

The Embassy Compound

It's Saturday and the Embassy compound children are out for clean private air and family activity on the lawns. Cynthia has homework to do, and I decide to spend the morning mostly in my room reading one or more of the unread books I've brought along and making a few perfunctory notes on our trip in preparation for the official report I will have to submit to USIA at some point. I join Bruce and Tad for lunch with an Albanian AID official who insists on treating us to pizzas at his favorite pizza parlor, an unpretentious place in a more than unpretentious part of town. The official proves to be jolly about many things—agricultural progress in particular—until we come to local politics, where irony takes over: all these so-called converts to democracy who were once ardent communists and who are now just as ardent fence-straddlers—"and that," he says, "includes our President Berisha." Maybe it goes with the office of president, I'm tempted to say, but I hold my tongue.

On the way home at siesta time, we call Greece from the one easily accessible public phone in town, in the lobby of the Hotel Daiti. I speak to Mary, Tad to her daughter Christina. I learn that all is as well in Athens as one can expect in a free-wheeling, ungoverned city at the start of July's dog days, and in any case, Mary is with our friends the Gilbertsons by the sea outside Athens eating fresh fish and therefore in good spirits. Christina is with her husband by the sea in Chalkidiki eating fried mussels and also in good spirits. Why do we in Tirana sound so solemn and so far away? Easy: we've just had a pizza lunch on a dusty street in a city where communication with the outside world is still anything but casual, and our sea is well out of reach to the west.

A knock on the door wakes me up from a long siesta: Cynthia reminds me that a gentleman named Dr. Emin Riza of the Academy of Arts and Sciences is due any minute to pick up a letter I've promised to deliver to him from Diane Katsificas-Gilbertson of the University of Minnesota, who worked with him recently on a symposium that explored much unfamiliar material relating to the Byzantine art in Albania. Mr. Riza's English-speaking daughter is to act as interpreter because his other language is French, and I don't trust my vaudeville version of French whatever his version may be. But Mr. Riza arrives without his daughter, perspiring, twenty minutes late because he had some trouble both getting to, and into, the Embassy compound. We try and fail to communicate reasonably in French, so Cynthia agrees to serve as interpreter and translates Diane's open letter for him. He thanks Cynthia, tucks the letter away, says something to me in Albanian, sees my frustration, smiles wanly at me, tells me through Cynthia to give Diane and her husband his best regards, apparently apologizes to Cynthia for being in such a hurry but, alas, has another important errand on the far side of the city, and then is gone: back as quickly as possible to what must seem a more plausible life outside this compound. The last time I felt so imprisoned by my language inadequacy was trying to make my way north through Yugoslavia on my college German after Tito first opened his southern border to Americans some forty-five years ago.

Piro Misha of the Soros Foundation and Albanian PEN arrives next, also perspiring but exactly on time and not in any particular hurry. In the aftermath of our lunch conversation—how many days ago?—my mission now is to see if I can work with him to bring about a meeting between Albanian writers, PEN members or otherwise, and their counterparts in Greece—not likely to be PEN members there, since the so-called Greek PEN Club is still a dubious organization despite the efforts of serious writers in Athens to open up its membership and make it act responsibly. Piro is ready to travel to Athens anytime such a meeting between writers can be arranged. I promise to help with that. And he wants to promote exchange between writers by way of more anthologies in translation. I'm with him there as well.

We end up talking about the recent history of writing and publishing in Albania, the problems of production, distribution, and international recognition, which strike me as only an extreme case of the same problems elsewhere. Piro is optimistic, things have begun to change, more good publishers are now coming on the scene—in Tirana, not Elbasan, he says glancing pointedly at me—and if there are fewer readers in general than in earlier years, the quality of what is published has improved. We part with the prospect of meeting again in Athens in early September if I can manage to rouse relevant friends there so soon after their long August vacation. When he's gone, Cynthia comments that Piro is a good man, intelligent, with the shrewdness or luck to have focussed on learning English well at the right time, but also a bit spoiled: he had a responsible job in state-supported publishing during some of the more difficult transition years. Bujar was not so lucky, she says, picking up on what she took to be a rather snide reference to our Elbasan publisher. I tell her that my heart goes out first of all to Bujar and what he's done, but I still find Piro the most accessible and cosmopolitan intellectual that I've met in Albania—anyway outside Elbasan.

TIRANA BY NIGHT

The *Blue Guide* warns that visitors of either sex should avoid wandering around Albanian cities at night, including downtown Tirana. I feel like wandering anyway, a weakness I have some nights just about anywhere, including New York City and Rio de Janeiro, where recklessness of this kind led me, my wife, and our PEN companions Karen Kennerly and Norman Manea, into a collective mugging a few blocks from our hotel which cost me my wallet with $500 in it and a pair of summer pants slit open from my side pocket to below the knee. In Rio we were told by the locals to travel by taxi only; here the word is to travel only in groups.

When Cynthia turns out to be busy for dinner, I go next door to see if Bruce and Tad are free to wander the streets with me. No such luck, but their hostess, Deedee Blane, asks me to join the Lansdales and her other guests for dinner, a group of visiting diplomats also out to see something of the town. We meet the new arrivals from the States, the Mortons and the Walkers, outside the Hotel Tirana, tallest of local buildings, rich in glass, recently spruced up so that standing in front of it gives you the illusion of being at the heart of any modern Balkan city. That illusion dies the minute we move on to look for our evening's designated garden restaurant several blocks away.

The buildings along the main streets are more varied and more solid than their provincial counterparts, but they have the same dreary faces, the same evidence of advanced age and indifferent neglect. And the streets are darker than they ought to be. Still, those walking the streets here seem even less threatening than the jobless citizens of Elbasan. We cover much territory without apparently arousing any more curiosity than a group of foreigners this large would be likely to arouse in some other Balkan city. The adults we run into mind their own business, and the teenagers appear to be fully into their own teenage life of lounging and courting, but here mostly by way of private gesture, without the aid of loud music or wild transportation. Even the beggars seem to have gone largely underground since the *Blue Guide* last went to press.

The garden restaurant is off on an unpromising side street, but it has the familiar Mediterranean virtue of a green canopy of growing things and some access to the night sky. The food is also familiar, but I've now had a day to build a responsible appetite. The talk from our new arrivals brings me up-to-date on things back home in the States: the Simpson case, Clinton on Bosnia, the relentless Republican agenda. Jim Morton and Julius Walker are retired ambassadors who, it turns out, have run into my brother Bob here and there over the years: the Middle East, Africa, Greece. Hearing about the assignment that has brought them to Tirana amuses me at first: they are part of a team that will help to train Albanian public servants in the subtleties of diplomacy. I wonder to myself how you teach that sort of thing to anybody, and as I hear myself thinking this, I remember how very often people have asked me exactly that about teaching creative writing. Through the course of the dinner it becomes clear that these two diplomats are old pros, learned in the game of nations and well versed in how to talk about it. I decide that they will find a way to teach what they know. Just as we writers, pressed into service, somehow find a way.

July 2

The Ambassadors' Brunch

Today I travel to Korca, and after so much time in the
Embassy compound, I'm ready to get back on the road, especially the road south toward home country. But first there is a
pre-July 4th brunch next door, and an invitation to that has
been passed to me by my companions for the trip south, who
tell me that there will be at least three ambassadors there, last
night's and the American ambassador to Albania, along with
other local foreign service personnel, a gathering of American
dignitaries as impressive as the compound has seen in some
time though meant to be entirely informal. I accept the invitation, and I try to show that I'm impressed, but that is a stance
that gives me some trouble—too many hangover memories of
such parties from my father's foreign service days in Greece and
Syria, though a lingering nostalgia for the audacious way I would
sometimes use those occasions, parents distracted, to escape
with somebody's daughter from whatever temporary residence I
happened to be living in for some late adolescent initiation into
what I then took to be exotic foreign sex. This sort of thing
soon convinced me that I was not made for the regular foreign

service, as my parents apparently hoped when they sent me to Princeton.

Before heading next door I have a parting chat with Cynthia. She tells me about the problems of handling applications for government grants to Albanians who hope to travel to the U. S. on an appropriate visa. "It's strictly a lottery," she says, "and I'm not speaking metaphorically." It turns out that in Albania selection by lot is the best way to avoid having to deal with those who try to earn a visa by bribery, political connections, insider favoritism, or hysteria. It occurs to me that, given the undying commitment to "mesa" in Greece and elsewhere in the Balkans —getting what one wants by approaching a friend in power or the friend of a friend in power—adopting the lottery system for dispersing governmental largesse might prove a giant step toward civilized behavior throughout the region.

Cynthia also talks a bit about the problems of regulating copyright in Albania where regulations are still fluid, and I counter with the problems of collecting royalties in Greece even when the copyright on a work is honored by a formal contract: some publishers pay according to the books they keep, others consider the distribution of a published work, with ample free copies to the author, sufficient recompense. One well established Greek poet, spotting a new printing of his latest volume in his publisher's bookstore window, expressed his surprise at this discovery and his gratitude to the publisher, with only the gentlest touch of irony, for having thought his poetry worthy of a second printing. "Maybe now there will be some royalties," he said rather meekly. "Royalties?" the publisher responded. "Are we going to stand here and talk about royalties or the beauty of your work?"

As I rise to collect my things I thank Cynthia for her hospitality, wish her well in her new assignment as African desk officer in Washington, and say (in a parting effort to show that I too can be honestly diplomatic) how impressed I was by the way she handled the Bujar envelope issue and by what I saw of the spread of periodicals and the selection of contemporary writing in the USIA library. Cynthia outlines what she has to read to keep up-to-date—more in a month, it seems, than I manage in a year. "I guess that's one benefit of your having been an English major," I say at the door, "though I've found over the years that once you start writing regularly, its hard to keep up like that, especially if you're a slow reader." Cynthia looks at me. "Who told you I was an English major? My doctorate is in German Philology." I try not to look too surprised. "Is that right? So how come they're moving you from Tirana to the African desk? Why aren't they sending you to a German-speaking post?" Cynthia gives me a controlled smile. "Are you kidding? I've never served in a German-speaking post. That's top of the line. How many women do you think get a post like that?"

The brunch is as American as you're likely to get on the 4th of July in the Balkans, and the ambassadors and their wives circulate and mix as convivially as anybody could want, but I'm uncomfortable after a while, eager to get going, and I find it increasingly hard to prepare a face to meet the unknown faces I have to meet. I end up in a corner of the rear patio off the living room with a double helping of punch between my legs. A tanned young man comes over to sit in the free chair next to me, puts out his hand and mumbles something I don't get, though I soon gather that he's somehow in the know, or anyway thinks he is, because he nods toward the far end of the patio where the current American ambassador, a bearded man of wide girth, is lighting his cigarette off another. "He's all right," the young man says, unsolicited. "Well-liked. With it. No ego problem. Not like the former one, old hat, profound believer in patron-client relationships, even worse. Ran the country. And knew it. He and Berisha." How could he run the country? I ask. The young man studies me with the kind of small smile that says, gently, you must be putting me on. "Bucks, of course, leks, whatever," he says. "American aid. How do you think we run countries?" I thought Berisha was much in control of things, I mumble. Too much so, some say. "Sure. Now. But not to begin with. Anyway, a lot of people would say that's how things have to be done in this country. They were run by somebody for fifty years or more without a break, so somebody has to run them now. You can't take that away from them overnight and hope to make them come out democratic is what they say."

Fortunately our hostess and driver for our trip south, Maura Schwartz, has an appointment deadline to meet in Korca and rounds up her passengers before the punch works to make me say foolish things to this young man. Maura is the country representative for VOCA (Volunteers for Oversees Cooperative Assistance), the American organization—partly supported by AID, partly by private sources—that sponsors programs to develop environmental and natural resources in emerging democracies, among these Bruce Lansdale's effort to set up agricultural secondary schools in Albania. She is from Connecticut, California trained, in her early thirties, good looking, sure of herself, fluent in Albanian, clearly a born leader who has a reputation for being good at handling both the Americans and the locals she works with. She also drives her Jeep Cherokee like a professional.

ELBASAN TO KORCE

I get the front seat because they tell me my legs are longer than anybody else's, Bruce and Tad get the back. From my high perch I have a clean view of the territory ahead as we come up to the familiar ridge that carries us beside deep ravines to Elbasan, the morning sun glazing the tilled fields in the valley below, those small carpet sections of wheat and tobacco and corn. And after the turnoff for Skanderbeg's sister's castle, the open view of blue mountains to the south, the grand Tomorit range that touched the poet in Edward Lear, and beyond that those dimmer mountain ranges finally fading out into what seems undiscovered country. I breathe easily, lie back and close my eyes, then open them again and sit up to take in all the sweetness out there for the last time. Then, just before the final turning above Elbasan, we pass a field on our left that takes me back to pre-war Greece: a wood-saddled donkey in the foreground, a load of bound branches beside it, a bit farther on two women in the field, each bent over hoeing a furrow. No sign of a man anywhere. No sign of the late twentieth century within reach of our car.

It takes a while, in view of Maura's appointment to meet friends in Korca, for me to warm my companions to the idea of stopping for just fifteen minutes to visit Bujar and take a quick look at the House of Onufri. "I can guarantee that in Albania there is no such thing as a fifteen minute visit," Maura says. I tell her that is a thing I know all too well, but nevertheless, this imaginative publishing enterprise that began with a single press and a table fork is something that shouldn't be missed. We bargain. With the help of Tad and Bruce, I get a half-hour commitment.

We find two people working at the presses in the House of Onufri but no Bujar. Flutura comes down from the second-floor office to say that Bujar will be back in half an hour. I explain that we have to get to Korca for an appointment and unfortunately can't wait for Bujar to return, but I'd like in any case to leave him a message. Flutura disappears to get me a piece of paper, and half way into my message I look up to see Bujar coming through the front door with his uniformed guard behind him. It seems a message has already got through to him. "But Mr. Mike," he says, hand extended. "What is this? You cannot pass through Elbasan without stopping to see Bujar. And your friends here. You must stay for lunch. What is your hurry after all?"

At that point I let Maura take over in Albanian. An hour later we are on the road again, having had a somewhat truncated tour of the House of Onufri, a visit to the office for a generous orange drink of some kind, a review of current Onufri publications, and a long goodbye—the last at my insistence, because I want to make sure I have what details I need to try and find Bujar an appropriate bookbinding machine in Athens. At the car door, Bujar pulls me aside and says, head bent, "About that envelope, Mr. Mike. It is not right." I give his face a pat. "Yes it is," I say. "Absolutely necessary." I climb in front and watch him standing there shaking his head. "Look at it this way," I say, opening the window. "You did us the favor of keeping us out of jail. I mean it." His look shows that he doesn't think I mean it at all.

The road out of town is new to me, but the streets still carry the same melancholy, the same feeling of life too long deprived. I look back once as we clear that last of the houses, and that is my goodbye to Elbasan. We come into more good mountain scenery on the way east to Lake Ochrid, through what Edward Lear found to be "most desolate and wild country," with—and here he anticipates George Seferis—"stern-wrinkled hills wall[ing] in the horizon, covered midway with oak forests." Now there are olive trees under cultivation rising from the valleys, and chestnut, pine, and acacia trees on the forested slopes, as varied as on Pelion and the high roads of the Peloponnese. We follow the Shkimbinit river a good part of the way heading south, lose it at some point and turn east again into a winding descent that brings us out to the lake and a view of surrounding hills that reminded Lear of the Abruzzi, me of the same hills in Northern Greece before two wars laid them bare. His drawing of the town of Ochrid on the far side of the lake shows a castle on a high rock above a field of minarets, with two costumed shepherds in the foreground. What we see on this side, as we hug the lake heading south, is the beginning of resort develop-ment, a cafe facing the lake here and there, boats lined up as though for casual rowing, and as we come into the town of Pogradec at the southern end, stretches of lake front set aside for sun bathers and young swimmers courageous enough to go for the dark still waters that stretch out far in front of them.

We stop for tea in Pogradec—unusually good tea—opposite a lakeside park that seems a bit sparse of children, accompanied or not, but with ample young men in groups walking this way and that or lounging on the grass. I remember that it is Sunday and wonder what else there might be in town to entertain men of that age on a free afternoon. What is missing in this park are the lovers. Where do they go on a bright day like this? The local black humor has it that in order to escape the aura or fact of puritanism and religious fanaticism, lovers hide out in any empty pillbox they can find. But maybe there are more tangible dangers lurking here that we foreigners don't know about. Or maybe the park is simply too open to the road and sky for the kind of sensual pleasures routine on a Sunday afternoon in neighboring countries.

Before we climb back into the Cherokee, Tad leads me to the lakeside to point out another of Enver Hoxha's summer villas, now a recreation center, a grand green and white complex some five kilometers farther down the shore, a construct that for many must have been more convincing evidence of the man's power than his worthless pillboxes. We are still short of time, so we don't stop to look into that dubious monument but head on south, coming out of hill country onto the great Korca plain, richest of Albanian plains in agriculture, now divided by privatization into narrow strips mostly of wheat, tobacco, and sugar beets. Here and there a stretch of poplars lines the road.

The *Blue Guide* tells us that the town ahead has a history of political activism, at one time a center for Albanian nationalists, then for monarchists, then for ardent communists, among these Enver Hoxha, who both studied and taught here at–is it plausible?–the French lycée. And the same kind of history carries on through the transition period. Bruce now tells us about a wild spree by townspeople and neighboring villagers who exercised their new freedom some time after Hoxha's death by cutting down row on row of their own two-hundred year old shade trees lining the road into town, then destroyed school buildings, green houses, dairy installations, God know's what else in a bizarre expression of liberated discontent that speaks eloquently to the psychological distortions that emerged from the reign of terror under this city's former French lycée teacher.

As we come into town, I get the feel of a more cosmopolitan pattern in the architecture and the layout of streets than what I've seen so far, also more evidence of recent civic care and some remnants of a wealthier tradition in individual houses to modify the usual concrete and brick facade of communal living. I look for signs of Seferis's ghost and the ethnic Greek element, once substantial, that apparently brought him here as consul before the war. I find little that is visible, though my companions tell me that it still abides in the local Orthodox churches and that one still hears Greek spoken now and then, even after the continuing exodus of ethnic Greeks over the border to the southeast.

Maura's rendezvous is at our hotel in the center of town, the Illyria, a very modestly upgraded version of the Hotel Skampa. Her friends are not there, so she hurries off to track them down. Our friends from the American Farm School in Salonika—Randy Warner, David Willis, Panayotis Rotsios, Archimedes Koulaosidis—have arrived for tomorrow's graduation ceremony at the two-year-old Korca school that was modelled to a degree on their ninety-year-old institution, created originally by an American missionary in his early sixties, John Henry House, who believed that the way to the soul was through the work of hands as much as that of minds. During the last twenty-five years of his life he began to change the course of agriculture in the northern villages of Greece by practical hands-on training while at the same time tuning the spirit first of young Bulgarian Christians and then of Greek Orthodox Christians who came to him for knowledge and inspiration. His son, Charles, took over from him for the next twenty-five years, followed by Bruce Lansdale for another thirty-five. My parents rented a house at the school before World War II, Bruce and I taught there under the Fulbright program during the last days of the Greek civil war, and my friendship with Bruce eventually earned me a place on the school's board of trustees. My image of the Farm School and what I say about it are thus colored by passionate devotion and prejudice, with the rose-tinting of nostalgia.

After a short siesta break, the Farm School visitors head off to a local taverna-style restaurant, guided by the group leader, Randy Warner, a resourceful and authoritative young woman, formerly on the staff of Alfred A. Knopf and the American PEN Center, now coordinator of the Farm School enterprise in Albania. Watching Randy's skill in handling the mix of Americans, Greeks, and Albanians since we arrived in Korca, I am struck by a conviction that whatever dubieties there may be about the changing character and dimension of official American influence in this country, the work of less official representatives such as Randy, Maura, and Bruce surely provides the best kind of assistance that America has to offer in our effort to help those who need and want our help, much in the tradition of the early Peace Corps.

Our group is now joined by the director and assistant director of the school whose graduates we will be honoring tomorrow before our return to Greece by taxi, apparently the only available public transportation to the border. The Korca school's director, Pavli Mikerezi, is a stocky, tufted, voluble man in his thirties, much admired for his energy and good humor by those who work with him: an Albanian Bruce Lansdale in the making, they say. Between the second and third courses in the taverna, Pavli is persuaded to bring out the guitar he's brought along with him, and he and his younger assistant, Ilia Fundo—handsome, shy, with a delicate tenor voice—begin to serenade the table with a full-throated medley of traditional Albanian songs. One of them sounds familiar. So does a second one, a pre-war Greek tune. Suddenly Farm School old-timers Panayotis and Archimedes join in the singing: Greek words to the same songs. I recognize the Greek original now and join in too as best I can remember. Pavli and Ilia are smiling broadly—a bit of deliberate cross-cultural harmony, it seems, to bring back a vision of better times. We sing on full-voiced in our separate languages. In the back of my mind George Seferis's ghost comes alive reciting a song he made up in 1946 on the model of a pre-war popular song, a way to tell the agony of things lost. The song speaks of a Circe's sorrow as her modern Odysseus sails away for home at a time when the "Soulmonger" called World War II comes in abruptly to begin its work of destruction and exile:

> Sails puffed out by the wind
> are all that stay in the mind.
> Perfume of silence and pine
> will soon be an anodyne
> now that the sailor's set sail,
> flycatcher, catfish and wagtail
> O woman whose touch is dumb,
> hear the wind's requiem.
>
> Drained is the golden keg
> the sun's become a rag
> round a middle-aged woman's neck
> who coughs and coughs without break;
> for the summer that's gone she sighs,
> for the gold on her shoulders, her thighs.
> O woman, O sightless thing,
> hear the blind man sing.

JULY 3

THE KORCE SCHOOL GRADUATION

Breakfast in the Hotel Illyria is lavish: pans of fried cheese, pans of fried eggs, plates of meat, baskets of fruit, and along with the usual hot drinks, fresh mountain tea. We linger until it's time to travel across town to the graduation festivities at the Korca Pilot Agricultural School. It turns out to be part of a complex of local schools—foreign languages taught side by side with agriculture—the buildings either saved whole from the earlier irrational destruction or newly restored. Boys outfitted in the school's colors are playing a demonstration game of basketball in the earthen courtyard outside the main entrance, now blocked by arriving parents and students of both sexes dressed in their holiday best.

The graduation ceremony takes place in the school library, packed with folding chairs. Director Pavli is on a high, darting here and there to greet people, introducing everybody to everybody by name, doing his best to keep things moving but not much worried about falling more and more behind schedule since the mood is clearly festive, finally, as he crowds people into the library and begins his account of the school's short history and its range of accomplishments, responding to the evident enthusiasm of his audience by allowing his pride to beam out clearly across the breadth of his perspiring face. Behind me I hear somebody say in Greek, "Unfortunately this school is going to lose that man because he'll be mayor of this town in a year. You watch. Especially if he keeps his guitar handy."

Bruce is next on the podium. He works with a translator, a good translator, both of them professional in their timing. Bruce, brushing back his remnant gray hair, begins with a Hodja story, first making sure that his audience knows what Hodja he's talking about. The story goes that the wise Hodja is served a great dish of liver prepared in a special way by his hostess. As he leaves the table he asks the hostess for her recipe, writes it down, climbs on his donkey and heads for home, stopping on the way there to pick up a slab of liver from the local butcher so that he can test the woman's recipe tomorrow. Alas, farther along the road, a great hawk swoops down and plucks the liver out of his grasp. Hodja is greatly startled, dismayed, rendered thoughtful. Suddenly he begins to laugh, and he laughs and laughs. "Stupid hawk," he says to the sky. "The recipe is still here in my pocket, safe and sound. What good is that liver without the recipe?"

The point today, Bruce now tells the gathered students, is this: farming is a wonderful life, and here you have learned to do it well, but it only works in the end if you have the right recipe. To illustrate his point, he asks the interpreter to bring up his props: a wooden rooster, a calculator, a candle. A graduating senior of distinction is called up front by Director Pavli, a red-haired young lady, academically first in the class, a relatively sexy version of Orphan Annie. Bruce hands her the wooden rooster and crows the Greek word for good housekeeper, "niko-keeeeer", first item in his recipe: maintain, with proper pride, a well-kept home. The young lady takes the rooster and, turning crimson, tries to keep it inconspicuously hidden behind her. Next comes the class basketball star, a spindling young man who walks up with the stride of assured fame. Bruce hands him the calculator, recipe item two: you can't manage a farm properly without knowing the cost of everything you produce. The young man puts the calculator in his pocket, then realizes it isn't meant to be a prize—not yet anyway—and holds it awkwardly at his side. And then comes Bruce's recipe item three, the candle, presented to what is surely the class actress, a slender brunette on the verge of being voluptuous: with the light of this candle, she will spread her knowledge throughout her community by lighting other candles from hers. And with that Bruce lights the candle. The young lady holds it out in front of her proudly like a torch, applause swells to fill the room, tears appear here and there, Bruce gives his interpreter a hug, and Pavli steps in, hands raised, to bring the occasion to a close. Tad leans over to me and whispers, "So many times, so many years, and Bruce still gives it his all, right to the heart."

The room is cleared, tables are set up, a reception begins in the heat of high noon. I go for the chilled wine, which is gone by the time I finish my glass, then I try the local version of raki, strong enough to discourage most, me included. I pick up a bottle of luke-warm beer and head out into the corridor for shaded air. I find an open window at the far end and lean out to see if there is the makings of a breeze. The air is still. People have begun to clear out, and a minibus has pulled up to take the visitors from Greece on a tour of the Korce school's model farm. Beyond the minibus there is a storage hut of some kind, and on its wall, painted in large white letters, I read "Piro/Lili." Good— some young lovers do come out into the open here after all.

The school farm is a limited enterprise, with a small herd of cows and a flock of pigs running loose to compete for grub with the free-ranging chickens. We are shown a long shed with an impressive collection of the latest farm machinery, recently unpacked and still waiting to be put to use, lined up beside a crude, geriatric tractor brought into Albania by the Chinese some years ago and evidently preserved here for amusement only. We are now called to the dairy for a demonstration. It turns out that a graduate of the Farm School in Salonika, Evangelos Vergis, currently a teacher at a junior technical college in Greece with an Irish Ph. D., has arrived here with the first milking machine to appear in this region of Albania. Those responsible for supervising the dairy stand around watching his sanitary preparations and the application of the machine as though observing the first heart transplant, and the sense of muted amazement carries through the milking, though the cow goes on chewing her cud as calmly as she has all her days and though the milk comes out of the machine the same color as ever into the same old milk pails. When the milking is finished and the machine disengaged, one lady attendant, clearly an old-timer, bends down and strokes the cows teats as though to tell her that it's all right, the operation is over and she has come out of it unharmed and unsullied.

To the Border near Crystal Spring

Some of our group now goes off to visit a snail factory owned by a Greek entrepreneur who imports snails mostly from East European countries, uses relatively cheap Albanian workers to clean them, packages them in Greece, then exports them to France ready for the table. Others of us choose to go back to the Illyria Hotel to check out and arrange for a taxi to the border, where another taxi will meet us on the Greek side, near the village called Crystal Spring, to take us to Salonika. On the way to the hotel, Evangelos reports that his review of the Korca school's herd turned up some sick cows—a bit alarming but not really surprising, he says, given the still too-casual hygienic procedures. Maura will see to it that word gets passed on where it should go, and Bruce will have another chance to follow up on the matter when he returns in September.

By the time we get our baggage together, we learn that lunch has been put on for us by the snail exporter: fish, chops, steaks, everything but snails ("You have to go to Paris for that," he jokes). I skip the fruit course and go out with Bruce to arrange for our taxi. We are hounded by a late teenage beggar who has learned enough English and Greek and Italian to pester us interminably in the language of our choice—or failing that, his choice. He's imaginative and varied in his pleading, but the old hand travellers standing nearby insist that he should not be rewarded: he's been around a long time, gathering in enough to make him the most prosperous of the unemployed in town, and he hasn't even got a family to worry about.

Our taxi proves to be another product of the former Chinese patronage in Albania and its driver a committed optimist. He agrees to take four of us to the border—Tad, Bruce, David Willis, and me—but no more, and we learn why before we're a block away from the hotel: the taxi has no shock absorbers, and its remnant springs raise a serious question that is hard to discuss internally because of the harsh noise of metal against metal at every slight dip in the only partially resurfaced road and the rattle of the taxi's return to equilibrium after every slight deviation from a straight path. And the brakes give off the sound of persistent coaxing.

It turns out that the driver—pinch-faced, unshaven, mostly toothless—has picked up a certain amount of Greek during his frequent journeys to the border or from some other source he prefers to keep obscure. During a moment of relief on a straight-away stretch, I ask him how old the taxi is. "What is how old? You mean how young. Just fifteen years. Maybe twenty. It is mine only ten years." I mumble that it must have become hard to get spare parts since the Chinese left the country. "What Chinese? I make the parts. Better than the Chinese." I suggest it might be time for him to make some new shock absorbers and springs. "Why new? The old are O.K. now because the road became new. Asphalt all the way." I am silenced by the man's unassailably inventive sense of time's progress and his tolerance of its passing.

The trip to the border is blessedly short. It takes us over familiar country, the landscape in the narrow valleys painted in the same bright yellow and in the same shades of green, from olive to cypress, that one finds in Northern Greece, the low hills mostly uncultivated, mostly covered with light yellow and gray brush, a patch of purple here and there climbing to a bare rock crest. As we turn east and head down to the border crossing, I see soldiers in uniform for the first time on some kind of patrol, and at the border we find ourselves facing a double barrier on the Albanian side. Above the near one, a large group of young men are lounging on the hillside, either waiting to be allowed to cross into Greece, or having crossed illegally and been turned back, waiting for transportation home. There is a line ahead of us at the passport counter. The bored Albanian official in his cubicle refuses to be hurried: everybody is equally suspicious, and all passports have to be looked through carefully, twice—that is, until he spots my American passport, which he shuffles through quickly, stamps on the page marked "Amendments and Endorsements," and hands back to me with the very subtlest beginnings of a smile.

I end up the first who walks into the no-man's-land leading to the Greek barrier in the distance, my mission to reassure our next taxi driver that we'll soon be on our way to the Greek village called Crystal Spring and what is bound to be the purest of drinkable waters. The one other time I took a last-mile walk like this on my own was in the opposite direction in the summer of 1950, the time just after Tito opened the southern Yugoslav border to Americans, and on that occasion Bruce and Tad stayed behind to wave goodbye and shout encouragement from their tensely well-guarded barrier on the Greek side of an altogether desolate passage into territory then unknown both to them and me.

On the way down to this more active crossing so many years later I could make out what I took to be the high Grammos range far to the south, home of the battles that brought the Greek civil war to an end in 1949 and that—in contrast to what Tito managed to initiate—totally separated Greece from Albania for close to half a century. As my moments between borders are about to run out, I find myself bringing these recent days of adventure and discovery to a certain conclusion by remembering how much evidence I've found that Albania and Greece are beginning to come together again—not easily, not without continuing suspicion—but perhaps inevitably. I think of Bujar's words at the start of my trip days ago: Let history lie in peace; we need our energy for the problems we have in front of us. That now seems to me the best road to travel between Athens and Tirana, especially with a stopover at the House of Onufri in Elbasan.

AFTERWORD

On that day of parting in July, 1995, when Buyar Hudhri
walked into the House of Onufri with his exotically uniformed
guard behind him, his attitude about his future was something
between cautious and optimistic. He had recently computerized
his publishing enterprise, and he planned to expand his business as soon as he could bring in more modern equipment.
That day he gave me the details about the kind of used binding
machine he hoped I might track down for him in Greece, and
there were prospects for other updated equipment by way of
Italy. His caution had to do with the still unresolved political
situation in Albania. With a parliamentary election coming up
in the spring of 1996, he wondered what Berisha would do to
keep his party solidly in power and what the opposition might
do in response to an expected manipulation of the electoral
process by those of the President's people in charge of law,
order, and much of the media. Since Buyar's steady income
depended on government printing contracts, he felt that questions of political stability and national solvency were essentially
linked to his enterprise, however much his heart might be in the
less profitable literary aspect of his work.

Buyar was right to be cautious, though that particular summer and the fall following ended with further cause for optimism. By the time I managed to track down an acceptable second-hand binding machine in an Athens suburb, Buyar had succeeded in ordering a more suitable one, along with other valuable equipment, by way of Italy on the basis—Tracy Cabanis informed me—of a loan partially underwritten by an anonymous gift from an American source in support of the publication of poetry. And at some point the House of Onufri also succeeded in signing a contract with Ismail Kadare, the most renowned of Albanian writers, for several books then in progress. What no one could have accurately predicted back in the fairly blissful summer and fall of 1995 was the dimension of the rigging that took place in the May, 1996, parliamentary election and the chaos that descended on the country after the collapse of the so-called pyramid schemes in the winter of that year.

The two-round May election was simply a fiasco. President Berisha, evidently fearing that his Democratic Party might actually be defeated, saw to it that the opposition Socialist and Democratic Alliance parties were denied appropriate campaign funds and were prevented from holding rallies in the more important gathering places such as Skenderbeg Square in Tirana and other major town centers. He also monopolized television and other government-controlled propaganda outlets during the campaign. After the first round of the election, foreign observers such as the Vienna-based Organization for Security and Cooperation in Europe (OSCE) reported that there had been serious irregularities in the polling process. The result in that first round was that Berisha's Democratic Party won 95 of the 115 contested parliamentary seats and the main opposition, the Socialist Party, won 5. That party, whose leader Fatos Nano had been sent to jail under Berisha on dubious corruption charges in the summer of 1993, boycotted the second round of the election. Berisha's party ended up with 122 out of 140 seats in the parliament, and the President now had firm control not only over that legislative body but over the judiciary, the police, and most of the media. At the same time, he lost the support of his greatest recent patron, the United States, whose representatives were reported by Reuter to have suggested that he "go back to the drawing board," while the Council of Europe recommended that the election be annulled and new elections held within eighteen months.

Berisha would have none of that. In any case, it wasn't his diminishing credibility abroad, however damaging, that finally led to his downfall but the perceived collusion of his government in the pyramid investment schemes and his failure to warn the Albanian citizenry about the dangers of such investment— some would say an understandable posture from a political point of view since the pyramid schemes were for some time immensely popular with the public and their managers were occasionally shown supporting Democratic Party candidates or appointees. It is also true that no clear warnings from Berisha's patrons in Europe or the United States arrived in time to prevent the final wound to the country's already failing economy in the winter of 1996-1997. It was rumored that one and a half billion dollars had entered the Albanian pyramids by then, sustained not only by private investors but evidently by smugglers dealing in drugs, oil, gun-running, and migrant labor. Under the "anarchic capitalism" of these schemes—which had already proven highly pernicious in one form or another in Romania, Bulgaria, and Serbia—people invested their savings at magically high interest rates (from 8% to 25% per month), and earlier investors were paid off by later investors, the early birds quickly doubling their holdings and going on to make a killing if they drew out their principal in time. But if they came into the scheme late and stayed too long—that is, after unknown agencies finally pulled the plug and the illicit trade fell off—they lost their total investment, because at that point some of the major pyramid "banks" simply ran out of money, much of which was presumably by then in the hands of schemers who had been in the know.

The London *Times* estimated that seven out of ten families in Albania sank their savings into the pyramids, in some cases their livestock, land, and homes as well. When thousands upon thousands finally realized that they had lost all their money in this way, earned during years of hard work whether in Albania or across the border in Greece, riots followed, especially in Vlora, Lushnja, and other southern towns. The riots spread north, the police couldn't contain the mob fury even in Tirana, prisons were opened, rioters raided government weapon storehouses, criminals ran free and armed themselves as did most ordinary citizens whenever they could, the cities and towns were now ruled by armed gangs looting the day long and shooting off their assorted weapons into the night. The *New York Times* reported that looters' booty in the remote mountain town of

Gramsh, site of the only AK-47 factory in Albania, amounted to some 110,000 assault rifles. This kind of booty became the source of a substantial smuggling enterprise, with many of the weapons making their way across the border over old trade routes into former Yugoslav Macedonia and the Kosovo area of Serbia.

During the March chaos a cross-party interim government was formed under Bashkim Fino of the Socialist Party, and in April a United Nations-backed intervention force of 6,000 European troops under an Italian commander and including a large Greek contingent entered Albania to safeguard emergency relief aid then on its way in and to help restore some degree of order. At one point marines in helicopters arrived on the broad lawns of the American Embassy compound in Tirana to evacuate most Americans. I spoke to Buyar Hudhri by phone during those days to ask him how things were with him in Elbasan. "Not good," he said. "I have put guards around the House of Onufri twenty-four hours, and these guards have real bullets. No business is safe here. So far they haven't bothered me because I have no enemies and they don't care about my books, but I have some good equipment. The computers, for example." I told him Christopher Merrill and I were thinking of returning at some point to witness the new elections that rumor had it were now inevitable and would be announced any day. I could hear Buyar sigh. "Don't come. It isn't safe. They could kill you to get your American passport. Or maybe even your American shoes."

After much domestic squabbling and strong advice from

abroad, fresh general elections were agreed upon in May and set for late June. Berisha promised to step down as President if his party lost the election. Few really believed him. During the spring chaos, Fatos Nano, the Socialist Party leader, escaped from prison, was subsequently pardoned by Berisha, and traveled to Greece on a semi-official visit. He became head of the allied opposition, and when the Socialists and their allies won more than two-thirds of the 155 parliamentary seats in the two-round election of June 29 and July 6, Fatos Nano became Prime Minister. President Berisha acknowledged the defeat of his Democratic Party. Leka Zog (or Zogu), the very tall son of the former King Zog who had come back to Albania from South Africa in order to campaign for the restoration of the monarchy, declared himself victor of the referendum on that question but was in fact also defeated both in the parliamentary elections, where his Legality Party received only 3% of the vote, and in the referendum itself, where he earned an unexpected 33%. Zog disputed the election results on an unfounded claim of rigging.

There was some suspicion that Berisha was using the royal pretender in an attempt to subvert the election count, and further suspicion grew when the President tried to appoint a loyalist to replace the deposed minister of the interior, this after ordering the elite republican guard to block approaches to Tirana—but the courageous interim prime minister, Baskim Fino, countermanded the President's orders and won the day. In due course, Berisha kept his word and finally stepped down as President to lead the new opposition in parliament, a move that surprised many (though perhaps not Buyar, who had told me two years earlier that he believed the President to be an honest man but not a good politician). A Socialist Party physics professor named Rexhep Mejdani, whose idol was Albert Einstein and who declared proudly that neither he nor anyone in his family had ever been a member of the once powerful communist party—unlike both Berisha and Nano—now became President of Albania.

Two months after the election, the border between Albania and Greece was again cause for worry, with armed marauders waiting on the Albanian side to rob anyone traveling north and sometimes crossing the border into Greece for a quick raid on their dispossessed countrymen desperately searching for work where it had once been available. But in the cities there were some signs of progress. The Tirana airport was quickly remodeled in keeping with its more advanced Balkan counterparts. Shops were again open in the capital, traffic more or less normal, and the streets relatively quiet. Most working Americans assigned to the country had returned to their compound or their former homes. When I called Buyar in late September to find out how things were in Elbasan, he said that his guards were still posted around the House of Onufri, though public security was better in his region and in Tirana than it was farther south, where the police were mostly drawn from local residents who were still afraid to confront potential enemies in their own community. But he had visited Korca and had found it quiet, as in former days. He also went to Tirana regularly now because he was planning to move his publishing office there while keeping his printing operation in Elbasan. And he was proud to have Ismail Kadare's two latest books on his list. "The trouble is, Mr. Mike, I don't have enough business." Why was that? I asked. "Because the government has no money." I said a government without money was indeed a serious problem. "For them and for the country and for me," Buyar said. "For me they are necessary, after all. And I don't speak about politics or about repayment of pyramid losses. Nobody in my family invested in those pyramids. We are not so stupid, after all. And we don't want the government's money as a gift. Only for the work we do."

I wanted to tell him that if the new government would follow his earlier advice to forget revenge, say by way of avoiding political purges, and thereby leave history in peace so that it could concentrate on the problems ahead, there would be room for hope. But given the problems in Albania—given the recent history—I thought that would sound rather hollow now, anyway coming over the phone from America (even if a number of high-level representatives of the new government were in Washington at that very moment soliciting much-needed relief funds). I told Buyar instead to save at least enough money to accept Tracy's invitation to spend Christmas in New York, where all of us would meet to raise more than one glass of wine with him and make him eat as much as he had made us eat in the old days. "Maybe, Mr. Mike. I don't know. What can I say? We'll see."

—Princeton, N. J.
October, 1997

REFERENCES

1. The quotations from Edward Lear's journal appear in *Edward Lear in Greece: Journals of a Landscape Painter in Greece and Albania*, William Kimber, London, 1965.

2. The *Blue Guide* referred to and quoted from here is by James Pettifer, A & C Black Limited, London, 1994.

3. The excerpts from George Seferis's poems are taken from *George Seferis: Collected Poems*, Revised Edition, translated by Edmund Keeley and Philip Sherrard, Princeton University Press, Princeton, 1995.

4. Useful background information for the "Afterword" was provided by Miranda Vickers and James Pettifer, *Albania: From Anarchy to a Balkan Identity*, Hurst and Company, London, 1997; *Albania*, The Economist Intelligence Unit Country Report, 2nd and 3rd quarter, 1997, London, 1997; and *War Report*, Institute for War and Peace Reporting, London, April-September, 1997.

OTHER BOOKS BY EDMUND KEELEY

FICTION

The Libation
The Gold-Hatted Lover
The Imposter
Voyage to a Dark Island
A Wilderness Called Peace
School for Pagan Lovers
The Silent Cry of Memory

NON-FICTION

Modern Greek Writers
(ed. with Peter Bien)
Cavafy's Alexandria
Modern Greek Poetry: Voice and Myth
R. P. Blackmur: Essays, Memoirs, Texts
(ed. with Edward Cone and Joseph Frank)
The Salonika Bay Murder: Cold War Politics and the Polk Affair
George Seferis-Edmund Keeley: Correspondence, 1951-1971

POETRY IN TRANSLATION

Six Poets of Modern Greece
(with Philip Sherrard)
George Seferis: Collected Poems
(with Philip Sherrard)
C. P. Cavafy: Passions and Ancient Days
(with George Savidis)
C. P. Cavafy: Selected Poems
(with Philip Sherrard)
Odysseus Elytis: The Axion Esti
(with George Savidis)

C. P. Cavafy: Collected Poems
(with Philip Sherrard and George Savidis)
Angelos Sikelianos: Selected Poems
(with Philip Sherrard)
Ritsos in Parentheses
The Dark Crystal/Voices of Modern Greece/Greek Quintet
(with Philip Sherrard)
Odysseus Elytis: Selected Poems
(ed. with Philip Sherrard)
Yannis Ritsos: Exile and Return, Selected Poems 1968-74
Yannis Ritsos: Repetitions, Testimonies, Parentheses
The Essential Cavafy
(with Philip Sherrard and George Savidis)

FICTION IN TRANSLATION

Vassilis Vassilikos: The Plant, the Well, the Angel
(with Mary Keeley)

OTHER BOOKS IN THE TERRA INCOGNITA SERIES

Aleš Debeljak, Series Editor

Volume I
Four Questions of Melancholy
New and Selected Poems of Tomaž Šalamun
Edited by Christopher Merrill

OTHER NON-FICTION FROM WHITE PINE PRESS

BACKWARD TO FORWARD
Essays by Maurice Kenny
176 pages $14.00

ASHES OF REVOLT
Essays by Marjorie Agosín
128 pages $13.00

TWILIGHT OF THE IDOLS
RECOLLECTIONS OF A LOST YUGOSLAVIA
An Essay by Ales Debeljak
86 pages $10.00

WHERE THE ANGELS COME TOWARD US
Selected Essays, Reviews & Interviews by David St. John
246 pages $15.00

AMONG BUDDHAS IN JAPAN
Essays by Morgan Gibson
158 pages $10.00

AT THE EDGE
Nature Essays by Douglas Carlson
98 pages $9.00

OUR LIKE WILL NOT BE THERE AGAIN
NOTES FROM THE WEST OF IRELAND
Essays by Lawrence Millman
210 pages $12.00

WHEREABOUTS: NOTES ON BEING A FOREIGNER
Essays by Alistair Reid
206 pages $10.00

AMERICAN POETRY FROM WHITE PINE PRESS

BODILY COURSE
Deborah Gorlin
90 pages $12.00 paper
Winner 1996 White Pine Press Poetry Prize

TREEHOUSE: NEW & SELECTED POEMS
William Kloefkorn
224 pages $15.00 paper

CERTAINTY
David Romtvedt
96 pages $12.00 paper

ZOO & CATHEDRAL
Nancy Johnson
80 pages $12.00 paper
Winner 1995 White Pine Press Poetry Prize

DESTINATION ZERO
Sam Hamill
184 pages $15.00 paper
184 pages $25.00 cloth

CLANS OF MANY NATIONS
Peter Blue Cloud
128 pages $14.00 paper

HEARTBEAT GEOGRAPHY
John Brandi
256 pages $15.00 paper

LEAVING EGYPT
Gene Zeiger
80 pages $12.00 paper

WATCH FIRE
Christopher Merrill
192 pages $14.00 paper

BETWEEN TWO RIVERS
Maurice Kenny
168 pages $12.00 paper

TEKONWATONTI: MOLLY BRANT
Maurice Kenny
209 pages $12.00 paper

DRINKING THE TIN CUP DRY
William Kloefkorn
87 pages $8.00 paper

GOING OUT, COMING BACK
William Kloefkorn
96 pages $11.00 paper

JUMPING OUT OF BED
Robert Bly
48 pages $7.00 paper

WHY NOT
Joel Oppenheimer
46 pages $7.00 paper

TWO CITIZENS
James Wright
48 pages $8.00 paper

SLEEK FOR THE LONG FLIGHT
William Matthews
80 pages $8.00 paper

WHY I CAME TO JUDEVINE
David Budbill
72 pages $7.00 paper

AZUBAH NYE
Lyle Glazier
56 pages $7.00 paper

SMELL OF EARTH AND CLAY
East Greenland Eskimo Songs
38 pages $5.00 paper

FINE CHINA: TWENTY YEARS OF EARTH'S DAUGHTERS
230 pages $14.00 paper

POETRY IN TRANSLATION FROM WHITE PINE PRESS

THE FOUR QUESTIONS OF MELANCHOLY
Tomaz Salamun
224 pages $15.00 paper

THESE ARE NOT SWEET GIRLS
An Anthology of Poetry by Latin American Women
320 pages $17.00 paper

A GABRIELA MISTRAL READER
277 pages $13.00 paper

ALFONSINA STORNI: SELECTED POEMS
72 pages $8.00 paper

CIRCLES OF MADNESS: MOTHERS OF THE PLAZA DE MAYO
Marjorie Agosín
128 pages $13.00 paper   Bilingual

SARGASSO
Marjorie Agosín
92 pages $12.00 paper   Bilingual

MAREMOTO/SEAQUAKE
Pablo Neruda
64 pages $9.00 paper   Bilingual

THE STONES OF CHILE
Pablo Neruda
98 pages $10.00 paper   Bilingual

VERTICAL POETRY: RECENT POEMS BY ROBERTO JUARROZ
118 pages $11.00 paper   Bilingual

LIGHT AND SHADOWS
Juan Ramon Jimenez
70 pages $9.00 paper

ELEMENTAL POEMS
Tommy Olofsson
70 pages $9.00 paper

FOUR SWEDISH POETS:
STROM, ESPMARK, TRANSTROMER, SJOGREN
131 pages $9.00 paper

NIGHT OPEN
Rolf Jacobsen
221 pages $15.00 paper

SELECTED POEMS OF OLAV HAUGE
92 pages $9.00 paper

TANGLED HAIR
Love Poems of Yosano Akiko
48 pages $7.50 paper   Illustrated

A DRIFTING BOAT
An Anthology of Chinese Zen Poetry
200 pages $15.00 paper

BETWEEN THE FLOATING MIST
Poems of Ryokan
88 pages $12.00 paper

WINE OF ENDLESS LIFE
Taoist Drinking Songs
60 pages $9.00 paper

TANTRIC POETRY OF KUKAI
80 pages $7.00 paper

AMERICAN FICTION FROM WHITE PINE PRESS

WHERE THIS LAKE IS
A Novel by Jeff Lodge
184 pages $14.00

I SAW A MAN HIT HIS WIFE
Stories by Mark Greenside
224 pages $14.00

THE VOICE OF MANUSH
A Novel by Victor Walter
276 pages $14.00

GOLDSMITH'S RETURN
A Novel by Terry Richard Bazes
288 pages $14.00

LIMBO
A Novel by Dixie Salazar
200 pages $14.00

WAY BELOW E
Stories by Patrick J. Murphy
230 pages $14.00

PRAYERS FOR THE DEAD
Stories by Dennis Vannatta
196 pages $14.00

THIS TIME, THIS PLACE
Stories by Dennis Vannatta
186 pages $10.00

DREAMS OF DISTANT LIVES
Stories by Lee K. Abbott
206 pages $10.00

CROSSING WYOMING
A Novel by David Romtvedt
263 pages $12.00

EXTRAVAGANZA
A Novel by Gordon Lish
190 pages $10.00

OTHER FICTION FROM WHITE PINE PRESS

THE LOST CHRONICLES OF TERRA FIRMA
A Novel by Rosario Aguilar
188 pages $13.00

REMAKING A LOST HARMONY
Fiction from the Hispanic Caribbean
250 pages $17.00

MYTHS AND VOICES
Contemporary Canadian Fiction
420 pages $17.00

THE SNOWY ROAD
Contemporary Korean Fiction
167 pages $12.00

HAPPINESS
Stories by Marjorie Agosín
238 pages $14.00

RAIN AND OTHER FICTIONS
Stories by Maurice Kenny
94 pages $8.00

FALLING THROUGH THE CRACKS
Stories by Julio Ricci
82 pages $8.00

THE DAY I BEGAN MY STUDIES IN PHILOSOPHY
Stories by Margareta Ekström
98 pages $9.00

HERMAN
A Novel by Lars Saabye Christensen
186 pages $12.00

THE JOKER
A Novel by Lars Saabye Christensen
200 pages $10.00

About White Pine Press

White Pine Press is a non-profit publishing house dedicated to enriching our literary heritage; promoting cultural awareness, understanding, and respect; and, through literature, addressing social and human rights issues. This mission is accomplished by discovering, producing, and marketing to a diverse circle of readers exceptional works of poetry, fiction, non-fiction, and literature in translation from around the world. Through White Pine Press, authors' voices reach out across cultural, ethnic, and gender boundaries to educate and to entertain.

To insure that these voices are heard as widely as possible, White Pine Press arranges author reading tours and speaking engagements at various colleges, universities, organizations, and bookstores throughout the country. White Pine Press works with colleges and public schools to enrich curricula and promotes discussion in the media. Through these efforts, literature extends beyond the books to make a difference in a rapidly changing world.

As a non-profit organization, White Pine Press depends on support from individuals, foundations, and government agencies to bring you this literature that matters—work that might not be published by profit-driven publishing houses. Our grateful thanks to the many individuals who support this effort as Friends of White Pine Press and to the following organizations: Amter Foundation, Ford Foundation, Korean Culture and Arts Foundation, Lannan Foundation, Lila Wallace-Reader's Digest Fund, Margaret L. Wendt Foundation, Mellon Foundation, National Endowment for the Arts, New York State Council on the Arts, Trubar Foundation, Witter Bynner Foundation, the Slovenian Ministry of Culture, The U.S.-Mexico Fund for Culture, and Wellesley College.

Please support White Pine Press' efforts to present voices that promote cultural awareness and increase understanding and respect among diverse populations of the world. Tax-deductible donations can be made to:

White Pine Press
10 Village Square · Fredonia, NY 14063